Archaeology and Text

Duckworth Debates in Archaeology

Series editor: Richard Hodges

Debating the Archaeological Heritage
Robin Skeates

Towns and Trade in the Age of Charlemagne
Richard Hodges

Loot, Legitimacy and Ownership
Colin Renfrew

Celts, Germans, Scythians and Others
Peter Wells

Archaeology and Text
John Moreland

Forthcoming

The Origins of the English
Catherine Hills

Early Islamic Syria
Alan Walmsley

Archaeology and Text

John Moreland

Duckworth

For my mother and father

First published in 2001 by
Gerald Duckworth & Co. Ltd.
61 Frith Street, London W1D 3JL
Tel: 020 7434 4242
Fax: 020 7434 4420
Email: enquiries@duckworth-publishers.co.uk
www.ducknet.co.uk

A catalogue record for this book is available
from the British Library

ISBN 0 7156 2998 0

Typeset by Ray Davies
Printed in Great Britain by
Bookcraft (Bath) Ltd, Midsomer Norton, Avon

Contents

We parcel arts and sciences into fragments, according to the straitness of our capacities, and are not so pansophical as *uno intuitu* to see the whole

Richard Baxter, *Holy Commonwealth* (1659)

Illustrations

Fig. 1. Archaeology and history on a 'Hawkesian ladder' [p. 14]

Fig. 2. Digging up texts in the archive room of the Palace of Nestor, Pylos (photo: Department of Classics, University of Cincinnati) [p. 17]

Fig. 3. Wigber Low (photo: Professor John Collis) [p. 40]

Fig. 4. Word, Image and understanding [p. 47]

Fig. 5. The Word as Image in Bradbourne church (photo: author) [p. 55]

Fig. 6. The Image – the Bradbourne cross (photo: author) [p. 56]

Fig. 7. Hans Holbein the Younger (1497/8-1543), *The Ambassadors*, 1533 (photo: © The National Gallery, London) [p. 101]

Acknowledgements

I would like to thank Richard Hodges, not only for asking me to write this book, but also for his support, advice and friendship over many years. Deborah Blake at Duckworth has been patient, encouraging and helpful. Jack Davis (University of Cincinatti) and John Collis (University of Sheffield) have provided important illustrative material. In Sheffield, my colleagues John Barrett, Paul Buckland, Paul Halstead, Glynis Jones and (especially) Mark Edmonds have supplied ideas, information and encouragement, and have been prepared to turn a blind eye when I was writing about archaeology and history instead of chasing paper. Mark Pluciennik, Alex Woolf and Vanessa Toulmin have been invaluable friends who have contributed immeasurably to whatever value this book may have. My biggest debts, however, are to Prue and Tomás who tolerate me and keep me happy, and to my parents Patsy and Kathleen for everything they have done.

Department of Archaeology and Prehistory   John Moreland
University of Sheffield
March 2001

1

Fragments of the past

The low esteem felt by classical philologists toward field archaeologists was a remnant of the medieval tradition by which those who dealt in Dirt were felt to practise the mechanical arts, while those who dealt in the Word belonged with the liberal arts. The liberal arts are still more highly prized in academic places than the mechanical arts; the Word is still generally felt to be more powerful than, as well as cleaner than, the Dirt (Vermeule 1996: 2).

The knowledge of fragments, studied by turns, each for its own sake, will never produce the knowledge of the whole; it will not even produce that of the fragments themselves (Bloch 1953: 155).

Fragments in the present

Modern scholarship fragments the past on the basis of types of evidence – archaeologists study objects, historians study words. In the Beginning, of course, there was only the Word, in the sense that the Bible contained the definitive account of human history. In the nineteenth century, however, a combination of research in geology, evolutionary science, history and hermeneutics relativised this text through internal critique and setting it beside other sources of knowledge (Andrén 1998: 45, 136-7; Appleby, Hunt and Jacob 1994: 45-7; Piggott 1989: 38;

9

see also Chapter 3). One of the consequences was the creation of 'prehistory', as it became clear that the world and humanity had existed before the creation of the Word (Andrén 1998: 136). Archaeology was the point of entry into this Word-less world, and for many prehistory remains the proper domain of the archaeologist (Andrén 1998: 1; Arnold 1986: 32; Clarke 1978: 10-11). History, by contrast, is commonly seen as concerned with more recent periods, those for which we have reasonably abundant written sources (see, for example, Andrén 1998: 138; Pyddoke 1953: 15; Tarlow 1999: 263).

This fragmentation of the past into 'evidential' epochs, and the associated construction of academic disciplinary boundaries, is to some extent confounded by the existence of 'historical archaeologies', a series of sub-disciplines based on the fact that people in the historical past continued to make and use artifacts which can be recovered archaeologically, and on the existence of written evidence from 'prehistory' – in ancient Sumeria, Egypt and Mesoamerica, for example (for the variety of 'historical archaeologies', see Andrén 1998).

Intimately associated with, and flowing from, this temporal fragmentation of the past is another, epistemological, one. All historical archaeologies have to confront the problem of the relationship between artifacts and texts. The relationship between archaeology and history was, until recently, akin to that between servant and master. The basic facts of history, the historical framework, and the 'important' questions about the past were all established by historians from the written sources (Arnold 1986: 35; Austin 1990: 11-14). The role of archaeology in the reconstruction of the past was restricted to presentation – it provided the objects which illustrated the pages of history (Moreland 1998: 95). This subservient relationship was articulated by historians and largely accepted by archaeologists. Marc Bloch was rather exceptional in the value he placed on archaeological method and on artifactual evidence (1953: 52-4). Most historians are more ready to accept Philip Grierson's contention that

> the archaeological evidence ... in its very nature substitutes inference for explanation. It has been said that the spade cannot lie, but it owes this merit to the fact that it cannot even speak (1959: 129)

or that of Moses Finley:

> it is self-evident that the potential contribution of archaeology to history is, in a rough way, inversely proportional to the quantity and quality of the available written sources (1986: 93; also Andrén 1998: 23, 126, 145; Francovich 1993: 51; Sawyer 1983: 44).

In essence, many historians saw the contribution of archaeology to the study of historic periods as tautological (Andrén 1998: 145, 179).

This perception of archaeology as the 'handmaiden' of history can be traced back at least as far as the seventeenth century. Klaus Randsborg notes that even the celebrated Danish antiquarian Ole Worm (1588-1654) would place greater emphasis on quotations from written sources than on archaeological finds (Randsborg 2000: 216). The English antiquarian Thomas Hearne certainly had the epistemological priority of written sources in mind when he wrote that 'Conjectures may be allow'd ... where there is no Inscription to direct and a greater Liberty of Fancy is allowable in such Cases than where we have plain History to guide us' (c. 1711, cited in Levine 1991: 228).

More recently, archaeologists have been urged to accept their subordination. Nicholas Postgate, a Mesopotamian specialist, has argued that his field will only progress if 'archaeologists ... devise their research and record their results with historical issues in mind' (Postgate 1990: 239; also Alcock, L. 1983: 57). Others have made the same argument by stressing the 'inherent' superiority of the written sources in the writing of History. Jean Bottéro asserts that the 'mute' monuments can tell us little about the people of Sumeria in the late fifth millennium BC – 'for lack of documents, we know almost nothing about them' (2000: 8), while Lawrence Duggan argues that 'words … will always remain our most precise … mode of communication. *Pictures cannot "speak" clearly, only words can*' (Duggan 1989: 251, emphasis added).

Although there are some signs of a greater readiness among historians, 'sometimes it seems in spite of themselves', to use 'visual artifacts' (Andrén 1998: 122, 141-2; Samuel 1991: 89), this negative perception of archaeological evidence as a source of testimony for writing History still persists. Many scholars (and especially, it seems, archaeologists) have commented on this, and most have called for a rapprochement between the disciplines on the assumption that this will lead to a fuller understanding of those societies that left material remains in both forms (Arnold 1986: 36; Geary 1994a: 45; Gojda 1991: 57; Moreland 1992: 115; Postgate 1990: 230). Few, however, have questioned *why* the Word has secured this assumed epistemological priority. Those who have generally content themselves with references to the greater academic ancestry of history (Arnold 1986: 32; Austin 1990: 13-14) and trace the source of history's dominance to the early nineteenth century institutionalisation of the disciplines (Andrén 1998: 120; 127-8; Burke 2000: 91).[1] Some link it to the logocentric world within which we live (Clanchy 1993: 185; Andrén 1998: 61-2; Ong 1986: 23), while others argue (entirely erroneously) that we focus on written records because they are 'the most abundant resource' for understanding the past (Briggs 2000: 397). It has even been implied that the use of writing is an essential aspect of our humanity, or at least of civilisation (Bottéro 2000: 66; Briggs 2000: 419; Vernant 2000: 149-50).

I, however, would argue that the roots of this fragmentation of the past are more deeply entrenched and that it is essential to expose these if we are truly serious about renegotiating and transforming the existing relationship between the disciplines. In Chapters 2 and 3 I will begin to excavate the roots of this division and uncover the source of the epistemological priority accorded to written sources, but for the moment I want to consider some of the ways in which the relationship between archaeology and history has been conceived.

The 'bottom dwellers'

In 1954 Christopher Hawkes constructed his famous 'ladder of inference':

1. To infer from the archaeological phenomena to the techniques producing them I take to be relatively easy.
2. To infer to the subsistence economies of the human groups concerned is fairly easy.
3. To infer to the social/political institutions of the groups, however, is considerably harder.
4. To infer to the religious institutions and spiritual life ... is the hardest inference of all (Hawkes 1954: 161-2).

In essence, Hawkes argued that the incomplete nature of the archaeological record means that only inferences about basic production and consumption activities can be easily drawn, and that the 'superstructure' of past societies is effectively beyond our reach (Binford 1972: 94).

Strangely, this position is accepted (at least implicitly) by many historical archaeologists who, assuming also that written sources provide access to the 'nonmaterial' aspects absent from the archaeological record, transpose it thus onto the relationship between archaeology and history:

Religion/ ideology	Elites	History
Social relations/ politics	Elites	History
Subsistence	'Peasants'	Archaeology
Technology	'Peasants'	Archaeology

Fig. 1. Archaeology and history on a 'Hawkesian ladder'

These archaeologists seem to feel that the 'inherent' constraints of the archaeological evidence limit the kind of questions they can ask. They further reinforce the rungs on the Hawkesian ladder by suggesting that the socially restricted nature of writing in early historic societies means that documents tend to contain little information about production or technology, and by finding in this (apparent) absence a place for archaeology in

14

the writing of History (Andrén 1998: 124; Lloyd 1986: 45; also below, p. 21).

The late John Lloyd argued that it is unlikely that archaeology could ever substantially address 'many of the fundamental questions about the past' – inevitably, those concerning law, politics, administration and so on (1986: 42-3; Bottéro 2000: 6).[2] Archaeology, he asserted, can tell us about production and consumption in Roman Exeter, but not about the social rules and regulations governing these activities (1986: 47). Similarly, the German medieval archaeologist Günter Fehring argues that the 'type of evidence with which archaeology deals' means that we can answer questions about technology, etc., and in this way 'contribute to complementary problems posed by the historical discipline' (Fehring 1991: 229; also Green 1998: 1). In like manner, Della Hooke accepts the Hawkesian ladder, and archaeology's subservience to history, in her claim that although 'archaeology ... is an unbiased guide', it is only the historian who can 'explore the period through the thoughts of those who actually lived in it' (Hooke 1998: xii).

Acceptance of disciplinary and epistemological subordination is not a purely European phenomenon. In North America we are told that, while we can talk about the *function* of imported Chinese porcelain, only texts can tell us what the objects *meant* (Curtis 1988: 21). The fact that the decipherment of Mayan hieroglyphics led to a shift in focus from the 'ecological foundations' of the culture to 'ideological and political explanations' is another manifestation of this tendency (Andrén 1998: 87).[3] Indeed, the ubiquity of the 'disciplinary Hawkesian ladder' is implied in the focus of almost all historical archaeologies on questions of technology, economy and social conditions (Andrén 1998: 120, 124). Sometimes its presence is hidden under the cover of the claim that, because of the availability of written accounts, historical archaeology is superior to prehistoric archaeologies in the reconstruction of past realities (for example,

Schmidt and Mrozowski 1988: 32). What is not acknowledged in claiming this 'advantage' is that it accepts that archaeology, in its own right, is incapable of writing full and detailed Histories.

Stephen Gould, the palaeontologist, has noted the existence of a similar hierarchy of esteem within the sciences (Gould 1991: 278). In a metaphor appropriate to his discipline, he refers to the subjects at its lower end as 'bottom dwellers', and notes that not only do they accept their lowly position but they go even further and 'act like the prison trusty who, ever mindful of his tenuous advantages, outdoes the warden himself in zeal for preserving the status quo of power and subordination' (Gould 1991: 279). The same could be said for archaeology's relationship with history, and it is noteworthy that archaeologists have been among the most vociferous in the clamour to confine archaeology to the lower rungs of the interpretative ladder (see Austin 1990: 13; Arnold 1986; Vermeule 1996: 8). Although not all historical archaeologists are happy to remain 'bottom dwellers' (see below, pp. 21-8), it must be emphasised that the implicit or explicit acceptance of this status by others has affected not just the way we (as archaeologists) contribute to the writing of History, but the very practice of archaeology itself.

Writing and archaeological practice

The priority assigned to the Word in the writing of History from the early modern period onwards (see Chapter 3) meant that early excavations were often focused on places mentioned in written sources, an approach perhaps epitomised by Schliemann's use of the *Iliad* in his search for Troy (Andrén 1998: 17-18; Alcock, S. 1993: 172-3). In the United States, early historical archaeology focused almost exclusively on 'sites associated with famous people ... [and] events' and 'sites of national importance' (Orser and Fagan 1995: 25, 28), while in modern

Africa and India there is a tendency to excavate sites and monuments referred to in contemporary literature (Andrén 1998: 78, 59). Leslie Alcock, an early medieval archaeologist, endorses this approach and accepts the subservience it implies:

> It seems to me axiomatic that the archaeologist who chooses to work in an historic period must recognise openly his dependence on historians. This dependence begins, necessarily, with guidance on the identification of potential sites (Alcock, L. 1983: 57).

The sites chosen by historical archaeologists were (and to some extent still are) thus dictated by a desire to *complement* the information provided in written sources. In some cases it was acknowledged that the archaeological evidence did not sit comfortably with the written account that inspired its recovery, but this did not normally lead to reconsiderations of the relation-

Fig. 2. Digging up texts in the archive room of the Palace of Nestor, Pylos (photo: Department of Classics, University of Cincinnati).

17

ship between the written and artifactual sources (Andrén 1998: 18).

Subservience to the demands of history is even more evident in those cases where the practice of archaeology is explicitly directed at the recovery of ancient written materials (Fig. 2). Here archaeology ceases to be a discipline in its own right and serves merely as a producer of texts to be consumed by historians and philologists. *They* then write History. This demonstration of abject subservience seems to be a feature of the early history of historical archaeologies in, for example, Mesopotamia, the Mediterranean and China (Andrén 1998: 44, 63, 116), but is not a relict of the past. Excavations at the Roman site of Vindolanda were to some extent dedicated to the recovery of wooden writing tablets (Birley 1994; Orser and Fagan 1995: 8), and there are still calls for excavations to recover more Mayan hieroglyphs (Andrén 1998: 116).

Where archaeology moved beyond the single site and into the region, there was still a tendency to dance to the historian's tune. In classical archaeology, many early topographical surveys were designed to reconstruct the 'political arena' within which the actions described in the documents took place, and some material cultural studies were directed either at providing examples of the objects referred to in classical sources, or at resolving linguistic problems in those sources (Andrén 1998: 121, 116-19). Such practices persist. Margaret Gelling has lamented the fact that archaeologists still use their limited (and sometimes fallacious) understanding of place-names in the location and interpretation of sites (Gelling 1978: 11-14), and both early medieval and American historical archaeologists still have a tendency to try to accommodate the archaeological evidence within frameworks of legal status presented in written accounts (Bragdon 1988; Schülke 1999).

In recent years, some historical archaeologists have emphasised the partial nature of the written sources, arguing that since (in early historic societies) they were produced by and for the elite, they have little to say about the activities of the rest of the population. This 'insight' has been taken as the basis for an argument to ignore or minimise the use of written accounts and to assert that only archaeology can produce truly 'objective' Histories (Arnold 1984: 6; Deagan 1991: 103; Hodges 1986a: 70). Such arguments are, in fact, very problematic, not least because of the assumptions that the early written sources had nothing to do with the 'lower orders' and that the 'democratic' nature of the archaeological record somehow renders it more objective (see Chapters 4 and 5). They have also had an impact on the practice of archaeology.

One of the most consistent tendencies in contemporary historical archaeology is the emphasis placed on its supposed ability to give voice to those 'silenced' by their exclusion from written accounts. Sarah Tarlow argues that historical archaeology has the capacity to 'make visible the invisible people of the past – the poor, the illiterate and those who were socially, politically or geographically remote from the literate and empowered centres of elite culture' (1999: 263; also West 1999: 8). This, in fact, seems to be a particular refrain of American historical archaeology (see Chapter 5), and Jim Deetz's assertion that the written record provides us with History as experienced by 'a small minority of deviant, wealthy, white males, and little else', while 'historical archaeology deals with the unintended, the subconscious ... [and] provides access to the ways all people, not just a small group of literate people, organised their physical lives' (1991: 6), is typical of its kind.

I will consider these claims more fully in Chapters 4 and 5, but for the moment I want to look briefly at an element of archaeological practice whose growth in recent years has been at least partially predicated on its claims to rewrite the 'silent majority' into History. The ability of *field survey* to locate the remains of the homes of the peasantry, as well as those of the

19

elite, forms the basis of such claims. John Lloyd, having mini-mised the contribution archaeology can make to the so-called 'big' questions (see above, p. 15), went on to suggest that it can address other issues, such as 'where did the Italian peasant live?' (1986: 48), while Graeme Barker argues that field survey allows us to study whole settlement systems rather than just those aspects 'which the ancient sources chose to describe' (1991: 2). A clear demarcation seems to be established, on the basis of the type of data, between the kinds of questions archae-ologists and historians are able to answer.

This differentiation has been made more acute by the recent tendency to link this archaeological practice to a rather singular reading of *Annales* history. The argument is that field survey data (and sometimes archaeological data generally) best an-swers questions relating to the medium (socio-economic) and long-term (environmental) structures of past societies (Braudel's *longue durée* and *conjoncture*), and that it is ill-suited to addressing the 'history of events' (*histoire événementielle*) (see, for example, Barker 1995; Hodges 1986b; and papers in Bintliff (ed.) 1991 and Knapp (ed.) 1992).

The desire to give voice to those rendered inarticulate by the socially restricted nature of literacy in past societies is certainly commendable. However, it must be pointed out that when field survey, particularly if read through Braudellian *Annalisme*, does give these people a voice, it allows them to speak only of certain things – of how their lives were determined by environ-mental constraints, demographic pressures, economic cycles and the routines of daily life. They are rarely allowed to speak of purposeful action, of meaning and of power (Moreland 1992). These are seen (implicitly or explicitly) as the preserve of the elite, who articulate their thoughts in the words of the written sources. Again, the disciplinary Hawkesian ladder is repro-duced and reinforced through archaeological practice.

1. *Fragments of the past*

In a challenging, and now seminal, paper, Dave Austin
pointed out that

> the archaeologist feels bound by the rules of historical
> practice laid down by documentary historians. ... [Archae-
> ologists] have been so trapped by the agenda set by
> historians and so weighed down with the paraphernalia of
> medieval history that we scarcely feel able to interpret and
> analyse in the modes of contemporary archaeology (1990:
> 13).

Tim Champion has referred to this as 'the tyranny of the
historical record' (1990: 91; also Arnold 1986: 35). What I am
arguing here is that this (rarely challenged or even acknowledged) tyranny also affects how, and in what contexts, historical archaeologists feel bold enough to practise their art. Too
often it is the case that an absence of written sources, or a
perceived absence *in* them, justifies archaeological intervention. As Anders Andrén perceptively argues (1998: 126), by so
confining (and defining!) themselves, archaeologists paradoxically bear out Moses Finley's assertion (above, p. 11) that the
value of archaeology is inversely proportional to the quality and
quantity of written sources. I would further argue that the
search for 'text-free' zones in the past, into which archaeology
can insert itself, not only reproduces archaeology's subordination to history but also fundamentally misconceives the role of
both artifacts and writing *in* History (see Chapter 4).

Fighting back with New Archaeology

As I have already noted (p. 16), there have always been those
within archaeology who have not acceded to the priority of the
Word. In 1715 Thomas Hearne argued that antiquities were
'the most uncorrupted Monuments of History ... [and] the best

21

authorities for correcting such Writings as have been corrupted' (cited in Levine 1991: 231); while the Danish antiquarian A.A. Rhode (1682-1724), contended that 'archaeological experience is worth more than the authority of Tacitus' (Randsborg 2000: 212-13). The idea that written sources are somehow 'corrupted' or biased persists and is used not only to create a room for archaeology within the mansion of history, but also in more assertive claims for the autonomy of the discipline.[4]

Dave Austin, for example, argues that the value of medieval documents has to be measured against the fact that they 'were originally created by the elite to meet the economic and administrative programmes of the elite' (Austin 1990: 12), while Joyce Marcus suggests that archaeology can be used to 'test' elements of the elite myth, propaganda, and history recorded in hieroglyphs (1992: 6-15, 445). Emily Vermeule, a Bronze Age archaeologist, contrasted the archaeologists' capacity to reconstruct past reality with the 'literary landscapes of the philologist, which are not factual but inventive' (1996: 10). Some archaeologists no longer overlook discrepancies between written and artifactual data, but instead take them as a sign that they should cast off their timidity, and seize the initiative to 'find and interpret what is written in the soil. [The archaeologist] questions the earth as the agent of history' (Hope-Taylor 1977: 309).

The first systematic questioning of the nature of the relationship between archaeology and history emerged, however, with the advent of *New Archaeology*. This archaeological perspective can reasonably be claimed as the first to take an explicitly theoretical approach to the discipline and to consider carefully the epistemological basis of archaeological claims to write History. Many historical archaeologists have noted, and lamented, their subject's generally atheoretical nature (Arnold 1986: 36; Cleland 1988: 13; also Chapter 5, below), and it has been argued that the 'certainty' offered by written texts contributed to this failure to take theory as seriously as prehistorians had done (Austin 1990: 30-1; Arnold 1986: 36; see also Hodges 1983: 25).

In the 1980s a small group of British medieval archaeologists sought to change matters and urged their colleagues to adopt the theory and method of New Archaeology (Hodges 1982; 1983; Rahtz 1983). This is not the place to discuss this 'new' approach to archaeology in any detail (see Moreland 1991a; 1991b; 1997), but we should note that it was not a monolithic school of thought, and that the ideas of Lewis Binford (its principal exponent) changed and developed (although not for the better) over time.

Binford, in a direct refutation of the Hawkesian ladder-build-ers, argued that our ability to generate knowledge of the past was not inherently blighted by the 'incomplete' nature of the archaeological record. Rather, he asserted, it was 'methodologi-cal naïveté' which impaired our ability to move from the statics of the archaeological evidence to the dynamics of past human behaviour (Binford 1972: 96). In a rather bold, if undeveloped, claim he suggested that the 'nonmaterial' elements of past human communities were not absent from the archaeological record but were in fact 'encoded' in the artifacts and arrange-ment of artifacts contained within it (Binford 1972: 23, 95).

The 'methodological naïveté' which hindered the release of the full potential of archaeological evidence could, he suggested, be rectified through the development of 'middle-range research' – the discovery and utilisation of 'Rosetta Stones' which would allow us to translate the 'static material stone tools found on an archaeological site into the vibrant life of a group of people who in fact left them there' (Binford 1983a: 24). Such observations could only be made *in the present*, and, he argued, in three contexts:

1. fieldwork carried out among living peoples
2. experimental archaeology

23

3. by consulting historical documents (1983a: 25-6).

It was proposed that, on the basis of this 'middle-range research', *objective* inferences could be drawn about the human activities in the past which produced the archaeological record existing in the present.

These were bold claims which, if acted upon, had the potential to transform the practice of archaeology and rewrite the relationship between archaeology and history. Archaeologists working in historic periods would be able to interpret their data through an established body of theory, produce real facts about the past, and thus free themselves from a slavish dependency on data supposedly contained within the written accounts. And there can be no doubt that, for some historical archaeologies at least, the claims of New Archaeology especially when combined with its associated systems-based thinking and emphasis on internal development, had a liberating effect.

In Africa, New Archaeology, with its emphasis on internal development, allowed colonialist histories to be challenged and rewritten (Andrén 1998: 77), while in North America it countered diffusionist accounts and 'for the first time placed native people on a equal footing in this respect with Europeans and other ethnic groups' (Trigger 1989: 315). However, it soon became clear (although not to all) that this early confidence in the 'liberating' effects of New Archaeology was misplaced. The emphases on system and process, and on the creation of 'laws', were revealed as profoundly ahistorical – they minimised the impact of purposeful human thought and action in the creation of History and neglected the variety of past human experience (Moreland 1997: 168-9). In addition, Binford later turned from the optimism of his claim that information relevant to *all* aspects of past societies *was* preserved in the archaeological record (see above) to a more mechanistic consideration of 'site formation processes'.

1. Fragments of the past

Of particular importance, in this context, is the under-standing that, in his 'Rosetta Stones', Binford accords a naïve, uncritical primacy to documentary sources which merely serves to reinforce archaeology's subservience to history. He sees them as guides leading us through and commenting on the past, and implies that they provide unmediated access to its reality (Binford 1983a: 26). David Clarke, an early British exponent of New Archaeology, seems to have held written sources in an equally unhealthy regard, contrasting them with archaeological data which are 'never comprehensive, never capable of supporting but one interpretation and rest upon complex probabilities' (Clarke 1978: 11). Bizarrely, then, even these major archae-ological thinkers situate themselves among the disciplinary 'bottom feeders', and archaeology once more takes its place on the lower rungs of the interpretative ladder.

The notion that written sources can act as a Rosetta Stone is frequently extended into the claim that historical archaeologies can act as 'laboratories' for testing general archaeological theo-ries (Clarke 1971: 18; Binford 1983b: 169). This refrain, with its unacknowledged implications (see below), has been echoed across the historical archaeologies. Anthony Snodgrass, a clas-sical archaeologist, specifically aligns himself with Clarke in maintaining that 'historically-documented cultures are a poten-tially invaluable testing ground of theories and models developed elsewhere' (Snodgrass 1984: 227; Hodges 1983: 25).[5]

Not all historical archaeologists accept these arguments. Barbara Little cautions that 'instead of truly acting as a labora-tory, historical archaeology often offers itself only as a confirmation of models already created and applied to other data' (Little 1994: 12), while Chris Arnold refers to the naïveté of those prehistorians who believe that the presence of written sources would allow them to 'test their own theories within an historic period' (1986: 36). Neither, however, really tackles the acknowledgement of archaeological inferiority which the 'laboratory' concept contains – Gould's 'prison trusties' are here transformed into laboratory attendants. More crucially, they (and others) miss the point that this concept is premised on a fundamental underestimation of the written (and the artifactual) sources.

One of the fundamental deficiencies of all historical archaeologies is that they have treated the documents and artifacts simply as evidence *about* the past. One of the fundamental points of departure for this book is the understanding that written and artifactual remains from the past were not created with the questions of future archaeologists and historians in mind (Austin 1990: 12; Burke 2000: 140; Collingwood 1961: 12), but were produced, and had efficacy in the production and reproduction of structures of power, *in the past* itself. Dave Austin is one of the few historical archaeologists to have grasped this point. Attacking the 'laboratory attendants', he argues that their role is based on a failure to appreciate that

> the very fact of documentation is an agent of transformation .... A society which documents itself is of its very nature a different form of society from one which does not (Austin 1990: 29-30, emphasis added; see also Beard 1991: 39; Goody 1986: xi).[6]

The text as an agent of transformation means that we simply cannot conceive of historical archaeologies as 'text-controlled laboratories'.

In treating written documents as simply another source of evidence, New Archaeology is guilty of a 'presentism' which pervades much archaeological thought, and this becomes more pronounced in Binford's later focus on understanding the archaeological record as it exists in the present. By the late 1980s, he went so far as to claim that archaeologists must face the fact that they do not study the past, they create it. What they study is the archaeological record. ... We are not ethnographers of the past, we are not sociologists, we are not historians in the humanistic sense of the term. We are scientists dedicated to an understanding of the archaeological record (1989: 51-2).

In other contexts some of this would be unobjectionable. It is true that we study the archaeology record, and that (to some extent) we 'create' the past. However, when such statements are situated in the context of an overarching concentration on the archaeological record *per se*, we can see how far New Archaeology has moved away from any consideration of the past in its own terms. This impression is reinforced by the repeated assertion of the claim, itself mimicking and reproducing the problems of the Braudellian structure of historical time (see above, p.20), that archaeology is best suited to the investigation of the 'macrotemporal scale of systems change', of a 'temporal scale virtually invisible to participants in any intellectually unspecialised cultural system' (Binford 1989: 52, 51).[7] Archaeology is seen as uncovering the processes which governed the lives of people unaware of their operation and ignorant in the assumption that they had some control over their own destiny. Historians and ethnographers, who are here subservient to an omniscient archaeology, study their puny efforts. The steps taken up the disciplinary ladder by archaeology, however, have only been achieved through the creation of a past almost totally devoid of humanity.

Despite the liberation felt by some, few historical archaeologists ever listened to the siren calls of New Archaeology. Some claimed to have been intimidated by its jargon, others said that they were practising it already (see Hodges 1983: 28); both were, in fact, only to happy to continuing leaning on the crutch provided by the written sources. Still others purposely rejected the New Archaeology because of its dehumanising and ahistorical perspectives on the past. Here I would argue that we should reject it also because, like the archaeologies it purported to replace, it does little (despite its vaunted early claims) to help us renegotiate the relationship between archaeology and history, to demolish the disciplinary ladder, and to claim plurality with equality (Gould 1991: 279).

Meaning in the past

One of the most productive trends in recent archaeological research has been the charting of 'object biographies', showing how the meaning of artifacts changes in different contexts. Nicholas Saunders tells how pearls, seen by Mesoamericans as 'materialisations of light, concentrations of cosmic life', became 'one of only a few (commercially) valuable items' when appropriated by European 'traders' (1999: 249). In the movement from one value system to the other, their 'voice' was silenced and they were reduced to mute participants in exchange.[8] In a similar fashion, Lisa Seip traces the biography of a Nuxalk ceremonial mask from its life as a physical manifestation of a supernatural entity, activated through ritual performance and the transmission of oral tradition, to that of an object of art in a museum. The once meaningful object was transformed into a specimen from a remote past, in a display 'presenting a non-Native perception' (Seip 1999).

These brief biographies show that material objects were indeed imbued with meaning and were active in the construction of social and personal relationships *in* the past (see Chapter 4). They also stand as a metaphor for the way many archaeologists and historians treat material culture. In their hands, what were once 'very significant possessions' with real meaning and efficacy *in* the past (see Hoskins 1998: 196; also Hall 2000: 13), are transformed into fragments to be measured, drawn, counted and typologised as evidence *about* the past. Modern scholars silence their voice just as effectively as early modern 'traders' and collectors gagged those of native American objects.

Two objections might be posed to this contention. First, it might be argued that material culture was *not* the bearer of meaning in the past. This idea is certainly implicit in the work of some archaeologists and historians, especially with regard to 'utilitarian' objects. The almost totally blinkered focus of most historians on the creativity of elites must suggest that they see little of any value in other cultural productions. So, when Charles Briggs, a medieval historian, suggests that 'literacy, reading and writing ... lie at the very heart of what it means to be human, this being the ability not only to think, but to communicate with others' (2000: 419), there must be an implication that objects were not good for thinking and communicating with (see, however, Geertz 1993a).

Too many archaeological, anthropological, and even historical case studies demonstrate the significance of objects in the production and reproduction of communities and identities to permit us to persist with this fallacy (see also Chapter 4). Edmund Leach, for example, points out that

> the members of all societies, complex as well as primitive, *externalise ideas* about the physical and metaphysical universes, and about social relations within their own society, *by making and manipulating artifacts* (1983: 243, emphasis added).

Nor are ideas 'externalised' only in the kind of monumental architecture which was the subject of Leach's paper. As Martin Hall argues, 'the material world was constantly implicated in identity and the expression of power, whether the domain was the everyday life on the farm, ... or the grand schemes of house

29

form, garden design and the layout of towns and cities' (2000: 26; see also Hoskins 1998: 196).

Others, however, while conceding that material culture was indeed a medium of communication and a bearer of meaning in the past, might argue that we are no longer in a position to read/listen to it. I would counter that we have placed ourselves in that position, both by uncritically accepting the epistemological primacy of the written word and focussing so much of our attention on the words on the page, and through the use of methodologies which effectively silence the object. I will develop this argument, and those above, in Chapter 4, and will there outline an approach to material culture which *will* allow us to hear its voice.

Janet Hoskins noted that different sentiments may be expressed in different discourses. Among the Bedouin, poetry is the language of dissent and subversion, and songs of lament provide the Kodi with 'a cultural space' in which personal feelings, publicly denied, can be expressed (1998: 134; also Hopkins 1991: 144 for Coptic as subaltern discourse). These observations are another reminder that a rapprochement between archaeology and history must take place. In focussing on only one discourse, especially one as socially restricted and as 'overt' as writing, or in seeing all other discourses through its lens, we deny ourselves the possibility of hearing and understanding *all* the messages which emanate from the past. We do the same when we swathe the object in theoretical and methodological bands designed only to increase its evidential value in the present rather than to reveal its efficacy in the past.

However, if we are to effect the much sought after (by archaeologists, at least) rapprochement, archaeologists *and* historians must both change their perceptions of the written sources. Despite the insights produced by studies of the 'implications of literacy' (see Chapter 4), many scholars still have a propensity to focus primarily on the evidential value of written sources in the present rather than on their efficacy and meaning in the past. I am not in any way suggesting that we should ignore the information contained in documents. What I am suggesting is that we should cease viewing texts as the '*pis aller* residue of a lost world ... [or] as purely literary phenomena, but [see them instead] as eloquent, historically contextualisable and contextualising artifacts' (Briggs 2000: 398). We should focus more than we have done on the fact that documents are not neutral epistles, that they are not disinterested bearers of information about the past. Like other products of human creativity, they were, in fact, active in the production, negotiation and transformation of social relations. More particularly, they contributed to the creation and reproduction of technologies of oppression – as well as providing new opportunities for resistance (see Chapter 4).

As I noted above (pp. 14-15), archaeologists frequently try to stake out a claim for themselves by locating so-called 'text-free' zones where they can ply their (self-)limited trade. One of the implications of the above argument is that such zones do not exist. In any society with even a moderately developed level of literacy, the power of the Word entangled even illiterates in its web. The so-called 'people without history' were both distanced from and captured by the records of the powerful (see, for example, Deagan 1991: 100; White 1987: 56). Nor is it the case, despite the arguments of those archaeologists who emphasise the 'incomplete' nature of the written sources (above, pp. 18-19), that texts confine themselves to the ideological and political structures of past societies, leaving archaeologists to resurrect the bones of the economy (see Hall 1993: 178). As crucial elements in elite power, written sources were very frequently concerned with ensuring control over production and distribution (Austin 1990: 30; Moreland 1999a: 647-50). When archaeologists and historians cease to impose their fragmentation of the past on the past itself, we may begin to understand it in something like its own terms (see Hall 2000: 16).

In Chapter 4, I will make some suggestions about how we might move in this direction. Now we must return to the task outlined at the beginning of this chapter, for I do not believe that we can ever seriously renegotiate the relationship between archaeology and history, between artifacts and documents, without a detailed understanding of just how the Word came to claim the epistemological primacy it still enjoys. We have to relativise and contextualise the Word.

2

Words and objects in
the middle ages

The habit of preserving some written record of all affairs of
importance *is a modern one ...* But it is so prevalent and
so much bound up with our daily habits that we have
almost forgotten how much of the world's business, even
in communities by no means barbarous, has been carried
on without it (F.W. Maitland (1898), cited in Clanchy
1993: 185, emphasis added).

Our literate world of visually processed sounds *has been
totally unfamiliar to most human beings*, who always
belonged, and often still belong to ... [an] oral world (Ong
1986: 26, emphasis added).

A direct link with the past?

In his recent *A Social History of Knowledge*, Peter Burke reminds us that 'when one inhabits a system, it generally looks
like "common sense" ' (2000: 2). We inhabit a logocentric world,
the world of the Word,[1] and for many it is 'common sense' that
words speak louder than things, that the written sources from
the past are more informative than those recovered archaeologically, since they represent the voices of the past speaking
directly to us in the present (see, for example, Bottéro 2000:

33

6-7).[2] It is sometimes conceded that the written sources can be ambiguous, but we are usually reassured that historians have developed 'methodologies' for dealing with the problem (Lloyd 1986: 43).

The archaeological artifact (the Object), by contrast, is generally presented as remote and silent. Even when it gains its voice through the mouth of the archaeologist, its meaning remains inherently ambiguous (for example, Lloyd 1986: 43; Sawyer 1983: 46). It will support only inferences, never conclusions. It might be used to address some of the more mundane (generally economic and technological) questions about the past, but never (what historians regard as) the 'fundamental' ones, never the essential questions that deal with the heart and mind of mankind (Lloyd 1986: 42; Bottéro 2000: 6; Green 1998: 1; also Chapter 1).

However, like most 'commonsense' interpretations of the past, assumptions about the 'natural' vocality of the written sources (the Word) and the 'inherent' dumbness of the artifact (the Object) in fact 'exalt to the level of the eternal observations necessarily borrowed from our own time' (Bloch 1953: 80). It is self-evident that the Word has not always dominated human discourse; its epistemological primacy is neither natural nor unproblematic. Rather, like much we consider to be 'natural', it emerged from particular historical circumstances.

In the following two chapters, I will try to locate this historical context. I will do this by tracing the ways in which people actually used words and objects in social practice from the early middle ages to the eighteenth century. The intention, by showing how things were in the past rather than imposing the vanities of modern academic fragmentation, is to 'defamiliarise' the Word, to produce that 'distanciation which makes what was familiar seem strange and what was natural seem arbitrary' (Burke 2000: 2).

The Voice, the Object and the Word

From the twelfth century onwards documentary evidence was increasingly used in administration, law, history and even in the canonisation of saints (Clanchy 1993; van Houts 1999: 37; Olson 1994: 59). At first sight, it might appear that this provides us with the context from which its present dominance emerged. Contemporaries certainly recognised its power. In the late twelfth century, Guy, Count of Nevers suggested that writing had been invented 'so that what we cannot keep perpetually in our weak and fragile memories may be preserved ... and by means of letters ... last forever' (cited in Le Goff 1992: 74-5). This apparent privileging of written over oral (and presumably other forms of) communication is, however, more apparent than real. Although more books were available, medieval society remained 'fundamentally memorial', and the book was itself seen as a mnemonic (Carruthers 1990: 8; also Walsham 2000: 118). Despite the relative increase in the presence of texts, the literate elites of the middle ages still worked orally; 'texts were not scrutinised so much as used as a record to check against memory. ... The scrutinised object was in the mind not in the text' (Olson 1994: 62).

As Brian Stock emphasises, we have to consider medieval texts in their 'full spoken *and* written context' (1986: 77). Even charters, among the most prosaic and mundane of medieval written documents, were *post factum* accounts of oral transactions recording the names of those who had seen and heard the proceedings (Camille 1985a: 27; Clanchy 1993: 252-3). In the middle ages, the distinction between the oral and written worlds was by no means as clear-cut as it would later become (Stock 1986: 77; Camille 1985a: 26; and Chapter 3 below). We can see this more clearly when we contextualise the actual process of reading and writing.[3]

In the middle ages, reading was 'a matter of hearing and

speaking, rather than seeing' (Camille 1985a: 28; also Noble 1990: 97). Thus, Margaret Aston refers to the 'acoustic properties of books' (1984a: 193; also Woolf, D. 1986: 185), and even the financial statements of monastic institutions were read aloud rather than visually inspected – 'the modern word "audit" derives from a time when it was the habit to listen to, rather than to see, an account' (Clanchy 1993: 267). Further, the 'consumption' of some texts differed dramatically from the way we read books. Monks were urged to 'eat the Book' and *savour* the words, not in order to acquire new information, but because of the divine wisdom they contained (Gellrich 1985: 22). Here reading was not simply a visual act. Rumination on the word meant that it was also 'a physical exertion, demanding the use ... of tongue, mouth and throat [as well as the eyes]' (Clanchy 1993: 269; Camille 1985a: 29). However, not all acts of reading (or writing) were commensurate with understanding.

For the most part, the activity of writing in the middle ages consisted of the making of a fair copy on parchment, from the transcribed words of the *dictator* (composer) (Clanchy 1993: 126, 271; also Noble 1990: 88).[4] Neither in the act of transcribing nor in that of writing the copy need the scribe necessarily have understood the meaning of the text. Although a scribe could write, he would not necessarily have been seen as a *litteratus,* a category reserved for those who could use Latin as a living language (Camille 1985a: 28; Briggs 2000: 411). Scribes were, rather, mediators between the spoken and the written worlds; through their practice, they embedded the voices of the former in the latter.

Until recently, the very existence of such voices in texts, and the fuzziness they create in the line which separates the oral from the written worlds, was underplayed. Now we are well aware of the paradox that, with the increased use of the written word in (and survival from) the middle ages, so the Voice of the spoken word gets louder (van Houts 1999: 5; Stock 1986: 77).

2. Words and objects in the middle ages

There may also be a gendered dimension to these Voices in the text. The writing of documents was normally a male activity. Elizabeth van Houts, however, demonstrates that not only were women repositories of the (oral/aural) traditions of ancestral and family memory, but also that such memories were frequently incorporated into written texts (1999; also Hamburger 1989: 163-4; Innes 1998). Although men may have written the texts, women too made History.

Brian Stock has suggested that the increased use of the written word during the middle ages resulted in a 'rapprochement between the oral and the written' (1983: 3; also Camille 1985a: 27). What seems to have escaped him, and most of those who now appreciate the presence of the oral in the written, is the fact that in the middle ages (or any historical past for that matter) writing did not enter and conquer societies in which the spoken word was the *only* form of communication. The people of the middle ages, as in all historical pasts, lived within a created world of objects. If we are to contextualise, and thus understand, the Word in the middle ages, then we must listen, not to the dialogue between the spoken and the written words, but to that between the Voice, the Object and the Word.

Something of this articulation emerges from recent considerations of twelfth-century art. When we consider images from the middle ages, and especially those which contain written material, our immediate reaction is to privilege the act of seeing – we see and read the image (and the words); we understand the image as a depiction of something in the visible world. Michael Camille argues, however, that in many cases these images were 'not so much an expression of the visible world, as of the spoken word'. The prominence of the latter was symbolised by the 'universal sign of acoustical performance' – the 'raised and elegantly curved index finger' (1985a: 27-8). Camille subverts our expectations by recognising the priority of oral performance even in a visual and written text – 'both text and image are

37

secondary representations, external to, but always referring back to, the spontaneous springs of speech' (1985a: 32). Such an understanding should encourage us to rethink our attitude to the rest of the material culture of the period (this art is, after all, but a distinctive element in the material world) and to see it for what it was at the time – the repository of accumulated memory and a vehicle for generating meaning in the world (see also Chapter 4).

Some historians do recognise the part played by artifacts (some inscribed with writing) – altars, swords, tombs, tapestries and reliquaries – in preserving and creating memories of the past in the middle ages (Buc 1997; Clanchy 1993: 254-60; Geary 1994b; van Houts 1999; Remensnyder 1995, 1996). The meaning of such objects was perpetuated and transformed through the stories told about them in both the spoken and the written word. The objects, the stories and the texts provided communities with an 'imagined past', with 'a common set of symbols that help[ed] create the boundaries delineating and containing the community or society' (Remensnyder 1995: 3). The objects offered tangible proof of a connection (real or imagined) with the past and of the veracity of the stories told about them. In the medieval past, the power of words would have been immeasurably diminished by their absence.

In common with many historians, however, those cited above tend to consider only the dialogue with elite material culture – with the objects of 'art history' (see, for example, Kupfer 2000: 615). Raphael Samuel has noted that this focus on elite symbolic capital has resulted, by a 'kind of return of the repressed', in the rehabilitation of 'history from above' (1992: 229). Moreover, it would seem to imply that only certain classes of objects could (and can) speak, and conversely that the majority of the population lived in an overwhelmingly phonocentric world whose transience places them beyond our grasp (see, for example, Camille 1985a: 36).

2. Words and objects in the middle ages

By failing to take seriously the likelihood that, although they had fewer possessions, the poor also constructed their lives in and through a plurality of discourses, that they too invested their memories in, and read them from, material objects, and that the manufactured and natural worlds also provided them with the bases for future projects, historians (and archaeologists) construct an inherently improbable hierarchy in which elites actively construct and assign meaning to the 'object world' and in which the lower orders react to this world in terms of passive 'motor-response' (see Chapter 1). They also deny themselves the possibility of understanding challenges to elite authority (which may, in fact, have provoked the display of symbolic capital) and so provide the latter with an unbridled power in the present which they may never have enjoyed in the past (also Chapter 5).

Janet Hoskins, drawing upon her anthropological research in Indonesia, provides a sane corrective:

It is not the case that people in other societies produce and consume objects as automatons, except for a few moments spent straying into the 'special expressive space' of art, myth, and ritual. ... The imagination works on objects to turn commodities, gifts, or ordinary utilitarian tools into sometimes very significant possessions, which draw their power from biographical experiences and the stories told about these (1998: 196).

What historians, even those who have been drawn to 'read the signs', forget is that we can recover these 'ordinary' objects archaeologically, and that by placing them in context we too can see them as 'significant possessions'. Just as people in the historical past did not rely totally on written sources in the construction of self and society, so we in the present do not have to privilege the written word in our attempts to access the

39

Fig. 3. Wigber Low (photo: Professor John Collis)

40

meaningful worlds they constructed – a fully contextual archaeology allows us to do this (see Chapter 4).

The failure of historians to take seriously the vocality of the
material past is illustrated by the fact that few (if any) of the
numerous recent historical studies of the use of the past in the
construction of identity in the past draw upon parallel developments in archaeology (see, for example, the papers in Hen and
Innes 2000; van Houts 1999; and Semple 1998; Williams 1998).
Here, stratigraphy and context reveal the interpenetration of
past and present, and the manipulation of the former in the
service of the needs of the latter, every bit as eloquently as the
art objects preferred by historians.

We have no account (spoken or written) of the stories or
memories about the Bronze Age barrow at Wigber Low, Derbyshire (Fig. 3), that influenced the decision of a group of people
in the seventh century AD to insert their recent dead into the
tomb of the 'ancients' (see Collis 1983). What we do have is the
fact of that event; we have the archaeological relationship
between the Bronze Age and the 'Dark Ages'. By inserting their
dead into the barrow, the organisers of the seventh century
burial collapsed, and sought to command, time. By making
their dead contiguous with those of remote antiquity, they were
making an eloquent statement, informed by oral tradition and
memory, about their relationship with the dead and their place
among the living. In uncovering and reconstructing that relationship we stand in the presence of those statements. We can
get some idea of the kind of statements contained within that
'text' by looking at contemporary analogies.

Sometime in the first half of the eighth century, Giselpert,
duke of Verona, entered the tomb of Alboin (leader of the
Lombard invaders of Italy in the sixth century) and removed
the king's sword. This was not a simple act of grave-robbery, but
a purposeful statement about the past and the present. In
effect, Giselpert 'was entering the otherworld, meeting with the

41

dead king, and returning to this world as his successor. ... By emerging with Alboin's sword he claimed the right to lead the Lombard people' (Geary 1994b: 64-5). The sword, the object at the centre of this tale, was not simply a killing machine. As an object from the otherworld (and from the past) it was the bearer and signifier of authority (Geary 1994b: 67). Similarly, the tomb/barrow was not simply the resting place of the deceased, but a point in the landscape where this world and the other-world, where past and present, intersected (also also Semple 1998: 118; Williams 1998: 103). As such the tomb like the sword, was laden with meaning, memory and power.

Although written down in the eighth and ninth centuries, these understandings of the relationship between the living and the dead, and of the role of place and artifact as points of mediation, had for long circulated orally and were geographically so widespread as to suggest a 'common culture' (Geary 1994b: 56, 65). They almost certainly informed the perceptions of the people who buried their dead at Wigber Low in the second half of the seventh century, and were thus embedded in the 'text' constructed there. Much as Giselpert did when he encountered Alboin and took his sword, they entered the past in the service of the present to protect their future (see also Buc 1997: 107-10).

In making this statement, in creating their text, the funeral party at Wigber Low had read the landscape and its monuments, and had added to them. The biography of the monument now contained an additional page, which, although drawing upon memories of the past, significantly renegotiated the way the story could be told. Just as oral traditions had informed the initial reading of the landscape and the decision to appropriate the barrow, so the seventh century insertion provided those stories with a new ending.

This, however, is not the last verse in the story, the final page of the text, for the irruption of the written word (in the form of

Christianity) into this landscape from the eighth century on-wards almost certainly significantly altered the way some read this monument. As Sarah Semple has shown, the Christianisa-tion of the landscape transformed barrows from points of articulation with the ancestors into places of evil. In the Chris-tian mind, they became 'the haunt of monsters, spirits and evil creatures' (Semple 1998: 123; also Roymans 1995). However, it is clear from the accounts of sixteenth- and seventeenth-century antiquarians that barrows such as Wigber Low long continued to be foci on which people hung 'an entire magnetic field of traditions, tales, images and rituals' (see Woolf, D. 1991: 171; also Thomas 1983: 2-5).[5] Despite the presence of the Word and of truth (see Chapter 3), these barrows continued (for a while) to speak of other pasts and other beliefs. As Amy Re-mensnyder has emphasised, objects were more than just 'pegs for memory' (see van Houts 1999: 93-120); they were active in the construction and transformation of 'imaginative memories' (Remensnyder 1996: 885), and they remained so even in worlds where the written word apparently reigned supreme.

This chapter begins the search for the 'primacy of the Word'. It should now be clear that we cannot find it in the middle ages, for the spread of the Word did not mean the silencing of the Voice or the death of the Object. Michael Clanchy notes that 'technical deficiencies' inhibited the usefulness of writing in this period (1993: 262, 263, 268). However, he also points out that the persistence of an emphasis on the spoken word, and on the material world, was due to the fact that they were *customary*; people were used to them. The power of the Word was not immediately apparent to everyone. In the transfer of land, for example, many would have seen no reason to write things down when the words of the transaction were known in the hearts of men and were embodied in the broken knife symbolising the conveyance (1993: 258-9).

The middle ages thus remained a world formed through a

constant dialogue between the Voice, the Object and the Word; the latter two deriving from, and referring to, 'the spontaneous springs of speech' (Camille 1985a: 32). Events in the later middle ages would, however, significantly alter the balance.

The Word, the Image and the Truth

In 1101 English bishops dismissed some papal letters ('the most impressive documents produced in medieval Europe') as 'the skins of wethers blackened with ink and weighted with a little lump of lead' (cited in Clanchy 1993: 261). However, as we have seen, writing and documents were increasingly prevalent in medieval society. As I will discuss more generally in Chapter 4, the spread of writing in the middle ages, and its valorisation, stems at least partially from its ability to fix words and trans- mit them unchanged across time and space. However, in the middle ages, as in many historical pasts, the power of the Word derived as much from its 'supernatural' connotations as its practical implications.[6]

In one of the forgotten rituals of the middle ages (dating from at least the eighth century), the consecration of a church in- volved a ceremony in which the bishop sprinkled ashes in two broad bands over the floor to create 'a great St Andrew's cross or figure X' (Thurston 1910: 622; Remensnyder 1995: 32-4). With the foot of his crozier, he then drew the letters of the Greek alphabet in one of the bands, and those of the Latin alphabet in the other (Thurston 1910: 621). The origins and meaning of this ritual, the connection between the church and the alphabet, stem (as Thurston points out) from the fact that 'the alphabet is to be regarded as symbolic of Christ because it is the expan- sion of the A and Ω of the Apocalypse' (1910: 629) – 'I am Alpha and Omega, the beginning and the ending' (Revelation 1.8). Elsewhere, John the evangelist repeats the connection between the word and the divine – 'In the beginning was the Word, and the Word was with God, and the Word was God' (John 1.1); 'For there are three that bear record in heaven, the Father, the Word and the Holy Ghost: and these three are one' (1 John 5.7). St Francis of Assisi took the association literally and collected every piece of parchment he came across because they contained letters and these 'are the things from which the most glorious name of God is composed' (cited in Gellrich 1985: 35). In the eighth century the writing-hands of some scribes were revered as relics because they 'relayed the Word of God' (Camille 1992: 24). In this Christian tradition, the alphabet was a sign of 'cosmological totality' (Drucker 1995: 87), and as such was imbued with immense power.

In fact the connection between writing and the supernatural long predates Christianity. For Mesopotamians, the written word was 'the eternal meeting place between the visible living and the invisible eternal' (Herrenschmidt 2000: 88-9, 108), while in ancient Egypt, hieroglyphs of living beings were mutilated so that they could not 'regroup themselves into dangerous words and phrases' (te Velde 1985-6: 66-7; also Frankfurter 1998: 279-80; Parkinson 1999: 132-9). Mary Beard argues that in Roman religion writing came to constitute relations between pagans and their gods, and that, for some, 'the text itself could *become* the word of god' (1991: 50). Writing also had real power in the world and was commonly used in the creation and casting of spells and curses (Drucker 1995: 65-9). In Judaism and Islam, the texts of the Bible and Koran respectively were divinely inspired (Niditch 1997: 79-82; Drucker 1995: 78). Belief in the capacity of words and letters to exercise real power in the world, through their intimate connection with God, persisted into the late middle ages and early modern periods in the Kabbalistic manipulation of letters and numbers (Eco 1997: 117-43; Drucker 1995: 129-58; Piggott 1989: 56), and, perhaps more commonly, in the incorporation of words from the Bible

45

into amulets designed to ward off evil or cure sickness (Thomas 1971: 33, 328-39, 598; Walsham 2000: 120).

For our purposes, however, it is important to dwell for a moment on the implications of the ideas which lay behind the 'alphabet ceremony' described by Herbert Thurston. Christ's claim, mediated by John, to *be* the Word led to the view that the *logos* was 'the very essence of God as the full extension of the universe – transcendent, absolute and ultimate' (Drucker 1995: 78; also Remensnyder 1996: 903; Wallis 1973: 12). This in turn laid the foundations for a belief

> in the transcendent power of language and the Word, or *logos*, more generally … a faith in the authority of language when it is the embodiment of Law, or Faith. This belief raises the validity posited in language to the level of Truth. … These notions … have a … no less effective legacy in the traditions of textual interpretation which appear in literary studies, historical studies and the like (Drucker 1995: 78).

Thus writing (the Word), was directly associated with Truth, and this association had its most immediate impact in theological circles (although, as Johanna Drucker notes, it also had an impact in the development of historical studies in the West; see also Chapter 3).[7] In the middle ages, Latin 'was the language of inscriptions precisely because it carried the authority of truth' and for the theologians it was 'the only medium of true knowledge' (Camille 1987: 34; 1985b: 134, 141-2). Within the monasteries of Europe, the belief developed that study and contemplation of the revealed Word of God provided the most immediate and direct access to the mysteries of Christianity (Hamburger 1989: 166). A spiritual and social hierarchy flowed from this understanding, since the inability of the *illiterati* to read precluded them from gaining direct access to spiritual

2. Words and objects in the middle ages

Truth. Instead, their contact with the supernatural was mediated through images – what Pope Gregory (590-604) had called 'books of the illiterate' (see Chazelle 1990; Duggan 1989; Hamburger 1989). Within this 'hierarchy of knowledge', it was

> only in these second-status signs of the vernacular, [that people] ... could gain access to the spirit of the sacred page. They must fight for scraps under the tables where learned doctors feasted on divinity (Camille 1989b: 128).

We can summarise the theoretical, and hierarchical, relationship between Word and Image as follows:

Word	Image
Direct access to God	Indirect access to God
Literati	Illiterati
Ecclesiastical	Secular
Elites	Peasants
Truth	Imperfect understanding

Fig. 4. Word, Image and understanding

This was the theory. In some places, at some times, it may also have been reality. However, in the course of the middle ages the absolute dichotomy between *literati* and *illiterati* was rendered problematic by the 'diversities of rank and education' which had emerged by the thirteenth century (Hamburger 1989: 163; Camille 1985a: 32), while the expansion of lay literacy and the translation of sacred texts into the vernacular threatened sacerdotal hegemony over 'the truth' (Camille 1989a: 126; 1985a: 39-40). In response, clerics ridiculed lay literates by 'expelling' them to the margins of their texts (Camille 1989a: 126; 1992: 26), and reaffirmed their authority over the Word by producing an illustrated Bible which 'has the open book again and again

47

displayed as a sign of the authority and hegemony of knowledge in its proper hands' (Camille 1989a: 126).

However, this Bible can itself be seen as another symptom of the blurring of distinctions between Word and Image. It was, after all, an *illustrated* Bible. As such it undermined the autonomy of the Word, but it was entirely typical of a kind of 'artistic' production in the middle ages in which words and images mingled promiscuously on the same piece of material culture. In most cases it is clear that the images are secondary to the written word (but see Camille 1989a: 112) – they illustrate the Word in much the same way that archaeology provides the objects to illustrate the pages of history.

Something of this sense of subordination also emerges from a consideration of words located in 'semantic enclaves' on images or other objects (Wallis 1973: 1). The antiquarian John Leland (*c.* 1540) wrote that the cross at Reculver in Kent

> hath curiusly wrought and paynted the images of Christ, Peter, Paule, John and James .... Christ sayeth *Ego sum Alpha et ω*. Peter sayith *Tu es Christus filius Dei vivi*. The saing of the other iii. wher painted *majusculis literis Ro*. but now obliterated (cited in Peers 1927: 250).

Here the basis of logocentrism ('I am Alpha and Omega') was incorporated within an image in an attempt to precisely define what was being represented. Such inscriptions on objects are 'narratives of specificity'. By telling viewers 'what they are seeing, ... what to see, [and] how to interpret that which is hidden inside', the Word is used in an attempt to fix meaning (Remensnyder 1996: 905; Camille 1985a: 33).[8] In the words of the fifth-century bishop Paulinus of Nola, 'the script may make clear what the hand has exhibited' (cited in Camille 1985a: 32). It is, of course, true that only the literate would have been able to read the inscriptions, but we should remember that the viewing of these kinds of objects was frequently a 'community experience', the meaning prescribed by the inscriptions being communicated by the *literati* to the *illiterati* (Camille 1985a: 32-3; 1987: 33; also Wallis 1973: 2).[9]

Part of the dialogue between the Word and the Object thus took the form of the use of writing in attempts to *constrain* the 'luxuriant polysemy' of the material world, and such attempts were not restricted to ecclesiastical objects. I have already referred to the new reading of the landscape which accompanied the Christianisation of early Anglo-Saxon England. In this case, the Word was deployed to transform the ancestors into devils, a sacred topography into one of demons, and ultimately to encourage people to read the landscape in terms of Christian notions of good and evil. Nor was the use of the Word in this way a purely Christian phenomenon. Livy's written histories provided the definitive account of a place and thereby restricted the memories it could stimulate (Jaeger 1993: 362; also Chapter 4).

On the one hand, this use of the writing to explain, define and limit meaning both stemmed from and reproduced the hegemony of the *literati* and of the Word. On the other, the fact that such inscriptions were deemed necessary opens a chink in the theoretical supremacy of the Word and lets in the reality of a medieval lived experience. This use of inscriptions was an admission of the continuing vitality of the object as the source and repository of meaning. The inscriptions were an attempt to contain those readings within the orthodoxy of the Church (Buc 1997: 115; Remensnyder 1996: 905).[10]

From at least the sixth century, images had played a prominent, if problematic, role in Christian worship (Belting 1994: 1-46). By the end of the middle ages, when the theological and practical dominance of the Word seemed assured, images had become so prevalent that scholars speak of an 'image explosion' (Camille 1987: 37). The problem posed by these images stemmed from the ambivalence of their relationship with the supernatural. In theory, they represented, and allowed devotion to be offered to, that which was invisible (Belting 1994: 42). The honour or veneration offered to the image was, in theory, passed on to the prototype (the 'being' represented) (Barnard 1977: 8). Veneration was offered to the image/saint in the hope that the latter would intercede with God to secure otherworldly salvation or the curing of some earthly affliction. Combined with belief in the efficacy of prayers for the dead, in Purgatory, and in the capacity of the Virgin Mary and the saints to hasten the passage of the soul to Heaven from that transitional locale, the cult of images in the middle ages was intimately linked with the world of the dead and the ancestors. The crucial point here is that these images were meant to be *indirect* means of accessing the supernatural: only the Word provided direct revelation.

However, despite the effort of Christian theologians, there appears to have been continual slippage between the signifier and signified, resulting in 'the fusion of image and prototype' (Freedberg 1989: 406). The consequence was that images ceased to be simply mediators between Man and God, acquired efficacy in their own right, and were 'constantly used for very tangible purposes, from the repulsion of evil to healing and the defence of the realm' (Belting 1994: 6, 44; Huizinga 1990: 165).

For many in the middle ages, representations of the saints were points of intersection between the natural and the supernatural worlds (Denton 1987: 20). For others, however, this conception of images transgressed the rather imprecise line between veneration and idolatry, and ran directly counter to the Word, in the form of the Second Commandment:

Thou shalt not make to thyself a graven thing nor the likeness of any thing that is in heaven above, or in the earth beneath, nor of those things that are in the waters under the earth (Exodus 20.4).

But the fact that such transgressions did occur, that the *illiterati* (and not just they) claimed *direct* access to the supernatural via images, says much about challenges to the primacy of the Word, and to those whose power and authority was based on hegemony over it. Despite the theological claim that transcendental truths were embedded in the *logos*, at least up to the end of the fifteenth century objects were still seen as points of entry to other worlds, and the Voice was still a prime creator of meaning.

The images of cult which adorned the churches and landscape of late medieval England were not fixed and immutable creations, whose meaning was constant. Pious donors would pay to have images renewed through painting, gilding etc. The images were thus re-created, and were re-read in the context of the seasonal liturgy of the Church. The memory of the gift was preserved in writing in the bede-roll (the list of benefactors who were to be prayed for in perpetuity), and in the hearts and minds of those who saw the re-newed image. Much as those who buried their dead at Wigber Low added to the text that was the burial mound, so the donor's name would be inserted into the stories told of the life-history and efficacy of the image. The memory of the individual gift was encapsulated in the layer of paint, that of the community was held in the layers which had accumulated over time. The late medieval image, therefore, was not just a means of communication with God and His saints; it was also a repository (and focus) of parish memory. It served to perpetuate the memory of the individual, and the community of the parish, in material culture, oral tradition and the written word (Denton 1987: 23; Duffy 1992: 494-5).

The iconoclastic attacks on the material world of Catholic belief, which took place from the sixteenth century (see Chapter 3), did not therefore entail simply the destruction of 'monuments of superstition'. They involved the eradication of a material world which connected the living parish community with its past, and which lay at the heart of its collective memory. Paradoxically, they reinforced the hierarchy of knowledge (the priority of Word over Image) which had been at the heart of medieval theology from the time of Pope Gregory (see p. 47).

As we have seen, landscapes were also bearers of memory, and they continued to be 'read' by the inhabitants of late medieval England. Prominent natural and man-made features formed the focal points of late medieval Rogation processions, which, in the perambulation of the parish boundaries, defined both community and parish (Hutton 1996: 278-87; see also Chapter 3). The prehistoric stone circle, the various trees, and the crosses which served as markers in the eighteenth century procession at Ashover, Derbyshire (Kerry 1897: 26-7), would have been resonant with meaning and memory for the medieval inhabitants of the parish. As Donald McKenzie argues, these objects 'may not make sentences but they are messages' (1999: 42), and they were read and acted upon in the past. Alluding to the historical specificity of the Word, and to its 'elevation to the level of the eternal' – core themes of this chapter – he continues to argue that we can only begin to read these messages if we

> think not of books as the only form of textual artifact, but of texts of many different kinds in many different material forms, only some of which are books or documents ... The argument that a rock in Arunta country is subject to bibliographical exposition is absurd only if one thinks of arranging such rocks on a shelf and giving them classmarks. It is the importation into Arunta land of a single-minded obsession with book-forms, in the highly relative context of the last few hundred years of European history, which is the real absurdity (McKenzie 1999: 41).

This 'importation' is simply one manifestation of a tendency, which we will encounter frequently in this book, to overwrite the past with the present. It is a tendency which elides the difference of the past and creates continuity through to the present. It overlooks the power of objects in a world in which the natural and supernatural interpenetrated to the extent that the former was seen as 'a pulsating mass of vital influences and invisible spirits', not all of them 'Christian' (Thomas 1971: 266). It was a world in which holiness could be 'physically located' and in which the possession, manipulation and veneration of objects and texts had material efficacy – and not simply in the religious sphere (Thomas 1971; Flint 1991). More importantly, in this context, it was a world in which the dialogue between Object, Voice and Word was not yet dominated by the latter, and therefore one we must fail to understand if we listen only to what *it* has to say.

3

The Word and the press

As I stood there with my hand raised, it was as if the dove perched there spreading its wings had become an open book. And the dove departing from me was like a book taking flight. And the grain the dove held in its beak was like a kernel of knowledge seeding itself through the world. This is the vision I saw. And against it I set the memory of scribes, and of the earthbound slowness of their labour, and of the books around them shut in cases, kept from the world by lock and key. It was then that I saw what I must do in life, to help words fly free as doves (Morrison 2000: 52).

The destruction of images; the triumph of the Word

For the Reformation ideologues, the images which adorned churches were worshipped, not 'venerated', and their response to this failure to worship *only God* was a 'religious revolution of ruthless thoroughness' (MacCulloch 1996: 365-6), an out-and-out assault upon 'a culture devoted to the visual' (Denton 1987: 23). As in all revolutions, an essential part of this one was the erosion of memory (Aston 1997: 168), and, in acts of iconoclastic destruction, the Reformers destroyed that 'in which the collective memory of the parishes was, quite literally, enshrined' (Duffy 1992: 480; Denton 1987: 23; Walsham 2000: 88). They replaced a material world with the Word of God (written in printed texts and spoken in sermons) and thus altered 'the balance of power between word and image which had held for centuries' (Camille 1987: 40).

The text of Ecclesiastes 5.1, emphasising the superiority of the word over the ritual of the Mass, is the only 'image' (apart from some early twentieth-century additions) to adorn the interior of the medieval church at Bradbourne in Derbyshire (Fig. 5). Its medieval heart has been ripped out; in the graveyard, the remains of a monumental stone cross (Fig. 6), shattered by iconoclasts in the late sixteenth or early seventeenth century, stand in memory of the absence of all the other 'images' through which the liturgical and community life of the parish had been structured in the middle ages (Moreland 1999b). At Bradbourne, and throughout England, an implicit belief in the real power of images was replaced with the (re-)assertion of the superior status of the Word (see above, p. 52).

Fig. 5. The Word as Image in Bradbourne church (photo: author)

Fig. 6. The Image – the Bradbourne cross (photo: author)

The image of a text in Bradbourne church, and the absence of images, stands as a monument to the success of the Protestant campaign to make the Word 'the only means of spiritual communication with God' (Camille 1987: 40). Just as significantly, however, this success is reflected in the Catholic Church's reaction to assaults on the material culture of their liturgy. This included a renewed defence of images, but with strict controls on what could be depicted (Freedberg 1976: 29; 1989: 369), and a renewed insistence on the primacy of the Word (see Chapter 2).

3. The Word and the press

It is important to note that the initial Protestant position was the rejection of *unacceptable* images. Bibles produced in the mid-sixteenth century were illustrated, as was John Foxe's *Actes and Monuments* (1563) (Collinson 1988: 116), and Alexandra Walsham argues that 'it was hybrid media combining text with image and sound which made the most impact on a still largely illiterate populace' (2000: 76; 94). This all changed around 1580 with the emergence of a 'logocentric iconophobia' which demanded the repudiation of *all* images (Collinson 1997: 282, 300; Woolf, D. 1992: 13). This 'ascetic totalitarianism' is manifest in the absence of images from late sixteenth- and early seventeenth-century English bibles (and other books) (Collinson 1997: 294, 296-7), and in the fact that inscriptions became more important than images of the deceased on funeral monuments (Thomas 1986: 112; Llewellyn 1996: 180, 195).

For Patrick Collinson, the transformations wrought by this second Reformation were almost total; and by the beginning of the seventeenth century 'the English people became a people of the book, and that book was the Bible' (Collinson 1997: 282; Hill 1993: 7). In this 'triumph of the Word', however, the technology invented by Johann Gutenberg in his workshop in Mainz in the middle of the fifteenth century was as potent a force as theological argument and iconoclastic assault.

The power of the printing press to turn thought 'into a flock of birds' and scatter it 'on the four winds, occupying every point of air and space simultaneously' was immediately recognised (Hugo 1978: 196; Morrison 2000: 52; Eisenstein 1983: 12). By the beginning of the seventeenth century, Francis Bacon had named printing (along with gunpowder and the compass) as inventions 'unknown to the ancients' which 'have changed the appearance and state of the whole world' (cited in Eisenstein 1983: 12; see Zagorin 1998: 35, 224; Guizot 1997: 196). In the late fifteenth and early sixteenth centuries this power was harnessed by the Catholic church to produce and disseminate devotional material (Duffy 1992: 77; Jardine 1996: 163-4; Walsham 2000: 78), and may have contributed to an increased piety in late medieval England (Ackroyd 1998: 76).

However, despite its use of the press to disseminate the Word, the Catholic church maintained the position that only the *literati* should have access to certain doctrinal materials; 'exegesis … [remained] the preserve of the clergy' (Walsham 2000: 90, 108; above, pp. 46-7). They also prescribed (through the *Index Librorum Prohibitorum* and the *Imprimatur*) what could be read, and who could read it (Burke 2000: 141-2; Eisenstein 1983: 160; Jardine 1996: 171-2). One consequence of the prohibition of vernacular Bibles was that lay Catholics were less likely to learn to read (Eisenstein 1983: 173), and Eisenstein concludes that the shift from 'image culture to word culture' was more compatible with 'Protestant bibliolatry and pamphleteering than with the baroque statues and paintings sponsored by the post-Tridentine Catholic church' (1983: 36; although see Walsham 2000).

Contemporaries saw real power in the connection between print and Protestantism. John Foxe, in his *Actes and Monuments*, argued that God used 'printing, reading, and writing' to subdue his adversaries (Slavin 1982: 4), and, overlooking the history of Catholic printing, saw every press both as a fortress against the Pope and as one of the mechanisms by which he would be overthrown (Duffy 1992: 77; Walsham 2000). In allowing the production and thus circulation of multiple copies of the Scriptures and reformist texts, Gutenberg's invention was seen as providing the Germanic north with the possibility of liberating itself from the thrall of Rome (Eisenstein 1983: 150-1; Hill 1993: 335).

The destruction of images and the spread of the Scripture in the vernacular were motivated by, and effected, a new relationship with God. Neither the image, nor clerical control over the Word, nor the sacred points in the landscape now served as

3. The Word and the press

mediators between this world and the next. Truth could be experienced immediately and directly in the Words of the sacred texts which could be read (or at least heard) by all – 'the private citizen had become articulate in the presence of the Deity' (Eisenstein 1983: 167). The mass-production of books, the increase in the levels of literacy encouraged by the new faith, and the new unmediated relationship with the Divine all contributed to an increasingly 'privatised' consumption of the Word, effected through the eye, rather than heard through the ear (Chartier 1989; but see Walsham 2000: 109-10). Further, it might be argued that, despite the emphasis placed on sermons, the mechanics of printing and the form of the product broke the bond which had connected the written and spoken words in the middle ages:

> Distance from the scribal hand, production in relatively large quantities, mechanisms of distribution far distant from the author and printer, refusal of subordination to a ritualised verbal transaction ... [means that] the printed word does not serve the spoken, but has a kind of absoluteness, integrity, and finality (Greenblatt 1980: 86).

Here we might suggest that we have located one of the defining moments, perhaps *the* defining moment, in the Word's rise to epistemological primacy. The twin forces of the Reformation and the printing press significantly devalued the importance of the material world and of the spoken word, if not in everyday life, then in their perceived importance in communicating *truths*.[1] The moment is perhaps encapsulated in a broadsheet, produced in 1625, depicting

> a balance in which the Bible easily outweighs a vast conglomeration of Catholic equipment: all 'the Pope's Trinkets' – beads, bells, crosses – and 'the Divell to boot'

59

cannot tip the scales in favour of 'falsehood' (Walsham 2000: 74; see also Collinson 1988: 99; Hill 1993: 11).

The triumph of the Word was not, however, total. In early modern England meaning and truth could still be communicated by other means – if to increasingly fewer people. In the early sixteenth century, Thomas More reaffirmed the power of material images, and attacked the 'literalism' of the 'heretics' who seemed to believe that 'goddes word were of none authorite nor worthy to be byleved, but yf yt were wryten in the bokes' (cited in Woolf, D. 1986: 171; also Hill 1993: 15). Even some dedicated Reformers, committed to the Word, regarded the 'mechanical press as the handmaiden of the pulpit' (Walsham 2000: 76; Woolf, D. 1986: 174). Perhaps more significantly, there are clear signs that printed works – including Foxe's *Actes and Monuments* – were read *out* and heard, rather than visually consumed (Woolf, D. 1986: 185). The seventeenth-century antiquarian John Aubrey's recollection that, as a boy, he 'did ever love to converse with old men, as living histories' (Woolf, D. 1988: 48) reminds us that the ear and mouth did not entirely atrophy with the increased use of the eye for the consumption of the Word.

An awareness of the importance of the 'visual' in the late middle ages, and of a continued belief in the seventeenth century that the ear was the 'pre-eminent' sense organ,[2] reminds us that throughout the historic past meaning and memory were not confined within words or objects on an 'either/or' basis. From the beginning of the historical past, human beings have understood and constructed themselves through an articulation of written word, material objects, and the spoken word. However, the relative significance of these discourses changed over time. In the pre-literate world of seventh-century Derbyshire, the truths contained in the act of juxtaposing the recent and the ancient dead in the burial mound at Wigber Low were consumed by the eye and by the ear, and propagated by the mouth. The connection between *logos* and Truth had been present within Christianity from the beginning, but was always compromised by alternative, unauthorised, and 'material' paths to the transcendent. The reality of conceptions of landscape in which wells and springs, rocks and stones were points at which the natural and the supernatural worlds conjoined, and the belief that images were more than just mediators between these two worlds, threatened the theoretical/theological primacy of the Word. The texts read by the eye were still not always composed of words, and the truths spoken by the mouth and heard by the ear were not always those of the *logos*. While the triumph of the Word in the aftermath of the Reformation did not mean the end of speech and the death of the material world, it did represent a major shift in the way in which human beings understood themselves and their past. While the conflict between the Word and Image was indeed a spiritual battle about the 'proper' way of communicating God's word and of communicating with God, it was also one which affected the ways in which the past was remembered, and what was deemed worthy of remembrance.

Words, objects and antiquarians

There can be little doubt, as Margaret Aston has argued, that 'historical studies were profoundly affected by the Reformation' (1984b: 314).[3] There were some who, while agreeing with the need for 'reform', decried the destruction of the past which flowed naturally from iconoclasm and iconophobia, and already by the 1530s 'the spectacle of physical loss ... motivated antiquarian researches' (Aston 1984b: 314; Parry 1989: 172-4). Camden deplored the destruction, and even the Protestant ideologue John Bale could agree that his was truly a 'wycked age ... muche geven to the destruccyon of thynges memorable'

(MacCulloch 1999: 206; Aston 1984b: 328). The mutilated churches and monasteries in the landscape of sixteenth- and seventeenth-century England were, for some, the source of a new nostalgia; and with this nostalgia, Aston argues, 'came invigorated historical activity' (1984b: 337; also Thomas 1983: 18-19).

This interest in material remains of the medieval past in the early modern landscape might, at first sight, seem to undermine the argument that the sixteenth and seventeenth centuries were critical moments in writing's rise to epistemological primacy. I would argue, however, that one of the consequences of the Reformation was a profound and long-term transformation in the way people *experienced* the landscapes within which they lived. A corollary was the opening up of these landscapes to *inspection* by others – including antiquarians.

Reformation edicts were designed to desacralise landscapes by, for example, 'dissolving' monasteries, tearing down crosses and making Rogation processions a purely practical exercise designed to keep the parish boundaries maintained and 'fixed in mind' (Hutton 1996: 281-2). These processions, once a ritual in which the parish constituted itself both in the communal action of walking the parish boundaries and in the expulsion of demons which it effected, were also affected by the process of enclosure (Duffy 1992: 136-9; Hutton 1996: 282; Johnson 1996: 44; Williamson 2000). Whether laid out by agreement or not, the hedges and ditches which now partitioned the landscape created new conditions for moving through and working within the world. They transformed the way it was *experienced* (Williamson 2000: 76-7; also Scully 1995: 18). In many cases the new field systems cut through the landscapes of yesterday as if they had not existed, and in so doing signalled the death of the past almost as dramatically as the iconoclasts' shattering of the pivotal artifacts of the Catholic faith. It is certainly significant that, like iconoclasm,[4] enclosure was intimately connected with 'new genres of writing, new practices of listing, new ways of expressing meaning through written discourse' (Johnson 1996: 78).[5]

The desacralisation and enclosure of landscapes not only represented a radical break with the past, but also created the conditions for seeing landscapes in entirely new ways. The destruction of the past (through dissolution, iconoclasm and enclosure) did not just cultivate a new nostalgia and a desire to preserve those elements of it that still existed; it also created the very conditions though which the landscape (and the material world more generally) was transformed from one of lived *experience* into (among other things) one of antiquarian *inspection*. One might go further and argue that not only was the *destruction* of the material past consequent upon the power of the Word, but so was the 'inspection' and *reconstruction* of this past by the antiquarians of the late sixteenth and seventeenth centuries.

While it is clear that antiquarians of the sixteenth and seventeenth centuries did collect, preserve, and study the 'relicks of bygone times', it seems that for most of them the testimony of the written word was an essential pre-requisite for arriving at a 'factual' understanding of the past. At the turn of the seventeenth century, John Speed lamented the fact that antiquity was a 'labyrinth of ambiguitie' caused by the failure of men in the past to record the events of their time (Woolf, D. 1990: 67; Levine 1991: 133). It is significant that, when he did use 'non-literary sources' – coins and inscriptions – they bore the imprint of the Word (Woolf, D. 1990: 69; also Momigliano 1990: 57-8). The artifact was used to fill in the gaps; its value lay in 'explaining and illustrating History' (Thomas Hearne, cited in Levine 1991: 233). Even those who used methods which most resemble those of modern archaeology were still constrained within the testimony of the written word.

In his exploration of the urns dug up in a field at Walsingham in Norfolk (published in *Hydriotaphia: Urn Burial*, 1686) Thomas Browne used his analysis of the fragments of cremated bone and of combs, tweezers etc. to establish the presence of women among the cemetery population. He also tried to determine the nature of some of the unidentifiable fragments by subjecting them to physical tests, and he contextualised the discovery within an ethnography of the burial customs of the Greeks, Egyptians, Hebrews, Persians, and Babylonians (Parry 1995: 251-4). Although it is now clear that these urns were Saxon, Browne believed them to be Roman and, as Graham Parry suggests, it was important to Browne that the urns *should* be Roman since this allowed him to 'invoke the illustrious classical names that give such splendour to his discourse' (Parry 1995: 251).[6] It might also be argued that these names served to legitimise this discourse, and thus show the implicit priority he accorded to the written word (see also Parry 1995: 257).

The point of this discussion of early antiquarian research in England has not been to diminish the significance of that research for contemporary understandings of the past, or for the development of the modern discipline of archaeology. Nor I am trying to judge these antiquarians by the standards of the early twenty-first century. There were things about the past which, before recent developments in archaeology, were simply unknowable to the likes of Thomas Browne. My point is simply to argue that, while the sixteenth and seventeenth centuries did see the emergence of a group of individuals dedicated to preserving and studying the remains of the past, their very existence was to some extent predicated *upon* the depredations of the Word, and their practice accorded a priority *to* the written word.

The priority attached by antiquarians to written accounts *may* be connected with the theological concept of the *logos* as

Truth (see Drucker 1995: 78; and above, p. 46). More immediately, their methods, practice and aims were to a great extent constructed within a more general understanding of the role of history in contemporary society. Early modern historians were not so much concerned with discovering the *truth* of what happened in the past as in using it as a source of moral exemplars for action in the present (Woolf, D. 1990: 12; Burke 2000: 182). This was connected with the belief that 'politics is the proper province of the historian ... [that history should be the] history of great men' (Woolf, D. 1990: 3-4). Thus in 1695, Sir William Temple urged historians not to concern themselves with matters that 'neither argue for the Virtues or Vices of Princes nor Serve for Example or Instruction to Posterity, which are the great ends of History' (cited in Piggott 1989: 23; also Levine 1991: 115). The material world of the past had little role to play in this kind of historical project; and this would have been especially true of medieval societies, dominated by monks and clerics, and offering few exemplars to a 'Reformed' world. In this history of the 'Virtue and Vices of Princes', the idea of using material (or even written) evidence to look at the more 'mundane' aspects of past human existence was rarely considered.

Collingwood has argued that 'prehistoric flints or Roman pottery acquire the posthumous character of historical evidence, not because the men who made them thought of them as historical evidence, but because we think of them as historical evidence' (Collingwood 1961: 12; Burke 2000: 140). This, however, is also true of much of the written evidence used by historians, both in the seventeenth century and today. The point is that early modern historians (like their modern counterparts) could treat such written sources as evidence for the historical past, but did not have the conceptual framework (at least partially because of the factors I outlined earlier in this chapter) to allow that the same might be true for artifacts. As Stuart Piggott argues, the requirements of an authority on the past were an accepted text by a named individual, the latter providing a comprehensible personality to validate the former. The past was a past of persons, history a recital of their acts written by others (1989: 36).

In summary, we can agree with Margaret Aston that the sixteenth and seventeenth centuries witnessed a burgeoning of antiquarian activity, and that the impetus for this stemmed (to some extent at least) from the spectacle of physical loss which they encountered in the landscapes of England.[7] It would, however, be naïve to see in this the beginnings of an 'archaeological' interest in the past, and it would be going too far to argue (as Peter Burke does: 2000: 41, 85) that this interest in 'things rather than words' represents the 'spread of a less logocentric conception of knowledge'. Even in the new world of 'detached observation' which was coming into existence in the seventeenth century, the Word encompassed and determined the Object, and harnessed its feeble voice to its stentorian roar to speak of the world of past politics, of the 'Virtue and Vices of Princes', of what were (both then and now) regarded as 'the fundamental questions about the past' (Lloyd 1986: 42). Crucially, the Word itself was determined by higher authorities, among the most important of which were the texts of 'The Ancient Authors' (Piggott 1989: 34).

The authority of the Ancients; the Supreme Authority

In the late seventeenth and early eighteenth centuries, medieval ('monkish') histories of Britain, and in particular Geoffrey of Monmouth's twelfth-century *Historia Regnum Britanniae*, came under sustained attack from antiquarians because of their incompatibility with the accounts of classical authors.

3. The Word and the press

John Woodward and Edward Stillingfleet dismissed the *Historia* because it conflicted with the accounts of Caesar and Tacitus (Levine 1991: 137, 147). The classical authors were not just used to destroy the Galfridian myth. Woodward, in attempting to refute John Aubrey's claim that Stonehenge had been built by native Britons, used Greek and Latin sources to show that the British had been a simple people before the arrival of the Romans and were thus incapable of having built such a complex and monumental structure. He concluded: 'Twere to be wisht that writers on these subjects would not rely so much on fancy and conjecture, but consult the Ancients' (cited in Levine 1991: 74).

In 1693 Dr Woodward acquired what he was convinced was a Roman votive shield decorated with images of the sack of Rome (Levine 1991: 151-2). For Woodward, as for Thomas Browne (above, p. 64), the object was a material expression of the connections being forged between Augustan Rome and Augustan England (Levine 1991: 155). More significant for my argument here is the way in which Woodward and others 'read' the images. As Joseph Levine notes, where antiquarians had been 'used to citing coins and inscriptions to explicate a passage in Livy or Plutarch, they now simply reversed the process and sought in the literary texts a passage to illuminate their new discovery' (1991: 162). As in much antiquarian research of the late seventeenth and early eighteenth centuries, the Object was thus englobed by, and incorporated within, the Word of the Ancients.[8]

Classical literature not only provided the framework within which the growing body of objects from the past could be interpreted, but in the minds of the elite it also formed the link between the glorious Roman past and the glorious English present (Levine 1991: 133; Parry 1989: 167). Further, this elite had been brought up within a system which believed that 'it was the ancient literary texts ... that best trained the political man' (Levine 1991: 115). The point here is that the connotations of

67

power and authority which had accumulated around the written sources in the secular world parallel, to a great extent, those derived from a Protestant faith in redemption through the truth of the Word. Antiquarians may have collected and displayed relics of the past, but they interpreted them, as they tried to live their lives, through the 'certainty' provided by words of the Latin sources. However, even these words were subordinate to those of the 'supreme authority' – the Bible.

In his *History of the World* (1614), Sir Walter Ralegh asserted that 'all histories must yeeld to Moses' (cited in Woolf, D. 1990: 46; Piggott 1989: 37). Not only did the Mosaic account in the Pentateuch predate those of the 'Gentile authors', it was based both on divine revelation and, since men in the antediluvian world were of much greater longevity, on the direct testimony of the Patriarchs (Hill 1993: 28; Levine 1991: 64, 190; Piggott 1989: 48). The role, and authority, of the classical authors only began where the Biblical account left off. This perception of the relationship between the Pentateuch and Greek and Roman authors allowed no room for 'prehistory' and meant that the comments of Caesar and Tacitus could be legitimately applied to the earliest inhabitants of Britain (Piggott 1989: 62).[9]

Like most antiquarians and 'natural philosophers' of his day, John Woodward directed his research at demonstrating the truth of Scripture (Levine 1991: 56; Appleby, Hunt and Jacob 1994: 44-5). While he might urge his contemporaries to 'consult the Ancients', the Bible was 'a sacred text, beyond criticism, let alone contradiction' (Piggott 1989: 37). It was the only *true* means of revelation; it exercised authority over other written sources and, as we shall see in a moment, it influenced how the latter were read and how meaning was extracted from them. For Woodward and his contemporaries, the Word reigned supreme.

The greater availability of the Bible in English, made possible by printing and Protestantism, contributed to higher levels of literacy (Hill 1993: 11); its centrality in 'reformed' life and the emphasis placed upon close reading contributed to a 'democratisation' of textual exegesis and its implementation in daily practice (Hill 1993: 15; Levine 1999: 26; Piggott 1989: 42). The availability of printed versions aided the application of this critical method to the classical sources as well, thereby removing the 'inconsistencies, implausibilities, and anachronisms that had accumulated over the centuries' (Levine 1999: 30; Momigliano 1990: 73) and revealing a pristine truth – the past as it really was. Moreover, while early eighteenth-century antiquarians such as Henry Dodwell aimed to expose the 'original' which lay behind, for example, Livy, they also sought to use that 'ur-text' as a means of accessing 'the primitive period before the times which classical narrative illuminates' (Levine 1991: 205). Thus a bridge might be created between the newly revealed truth of the 'prophane authours' and the truth of the Bible. Word met word and the truth of the past was revealed. For most historians and antiquarians of the sixteenth to eighteenth centuries, there was, literally, nothing outside the text.

Sola Scriptura?

Print and Protestantism were not the only factors transforming peoples' attitudes to themselves and to the past.[10] In a more comprehensive account, I would have explored the great importance of the Enlightenment and of the 'scientific revolution' (see, most recently, Porter 2000). But even here we should acknowledge that the ability to produce and disseminate multiple copies of the same work in exactly the same form immeasurably aided the process of scrutiny and comparison; indeed many of the scientific and intellectual achievements of the eighteenth century were dependent on the press (Porter 2000: 72-95; also Eisenstein 1983: 187-254).

Equally, we should not imagine that the association I have

sketched between Protestantism, the press and the primacy of the Word in the construction of the past means that Catholics were entirely excluded from the new world of letters. I have already noted the early use of the press to produce devotional material for the Catholic Church, and Alexandra Walsham (2000) has highlighted the continuing importance of printed works both for the liturgy and for the self-identity of adherents to the traditional faith.[11] Similarly, Reformationist histories of England were not the only ones constructed in the sixteenth and seventeenth centuries. Catholics too turned to, and rewrote the past in the light of their current needs (Thomas 1983: 20, 12; Walsham 2000: 99; more generally, see Momigliano 1990: 74-5). This Catholic use of the written word should come as no surprise. The Word had been already been beatified by the theologians of the middle ages; print and Protestantism were simply (but importantly) agents in its canonisation.

However, despite the evidence for Catholic bibliolatry, there do seem to be grounds for maintaining that the link between print, the Word and Protestantism had important effects on the ways in which the past (and the evidence from the past) was perceived. Johanna Drucker argues that the connection posited between *logos* and truth affected historical studies (1995: 78; above, p. 46), while Arnaldo Momigliano cautiously suggests that, within seventeenth-century antiquarianism, 'Catholics came to rely rather more than ... Protestants on inscriptions and coins and archaeological evidence' (1990: 73; also Woolf, D. 1992: 11-14). Similarly, Daniel Woolf refers to the 'documentary puritanism which by now fired the souls of historians and antiquarians' (Woolf, D. 1988: 51). Importantly, contemporary writers demonstrate an awareness of the connection between the reformed faith and primacy of the written word. Thus in 1772 Charles Davy linked his belief that the alphabet had been invented in the Sinai 'to inscribe the Decalogue of Moses' to the prohibition against graven images contained in the Second

Commandment (Drucker 1995: 211). *Sola Scriptura* might have
been the motto for this age (Hill 1993: 342). While it should be
obvious from our own experience and from our understanding
of the past that this did not mean the death of the Object or the
silencing of the Voice (but see below, pp. 72-3), what it did mean
was that the written source, as the bearer of meaning and as
the ultimate arbiter of truth, was accorded a renewed and
lasting primacy over other discourses.

Silencing the Voice

The iconoclasts who destroyed the cross at Bradbourne and
those (perhaps the same people) who created the images of the
Word inside the church there were almost certainly motivated
by a devotion to the Word (Figs 5 and 6).[12] They read the Bible,
listened to the sermons and talked to each other about their
meaning. Moreover, their lives were increasingly entangled in
the webs created by the written instructions and demands
which were part and parcel of living in an early modern state.
However, they did not cease to create and live in a meaningful
material world. The houses they lived in, the clothes they wore
and the churches in which they worshipped were all expressive
of their perceptions of themselves and of the world in which
they lived (see, for example, MacCulloch 1991: 13-14; 1999:
158-63). If they were true to the Word, the meaning of the
landscape which surrounded them and within which they lived
and worked would have been utterly transformed. Its monuments (including the barrow at Wigber Low) and natural features would now have generated stories radically different from
those told a few generations earlier.

For those who tried to maintain their faith, this same evidence – the fragments of the cross, the absence of the
rood-screen, the plain windows, the 'rearrangement' of the internal space of the church, and the walls stretching across the

71

landscape – would have evoked very different memories. No doubt many of the stories told would have been infused with a nostalgia more bitter than that which prompted antiquarians to recover, record and reconstruct their past. Like the antiquarians, these parishioners may have felt that they were living in a denuded material world; but it was still a meaningful one. It is not impossible to imagine that, even among these recusants, the Word (in certain forms) was not just tolerated or even resisted, but was actively sought out and consumed, either as a substitute for images or (more provocatively) openly read during Protestant services (see Walsham 2000: 112-13). In Bradbourne, as in many rural parishes of England, both reformers and recusants still (if differently) lived in and through Voice, Word and Object. However, as I have already remarked, there can be little doubt that, in terms of their role in the writing of History, the relationship between these discourses had dramatically changed.

Peter Burke has show that 'traditional knowledge' (communicated orally) was in many cases incorporated into the new scientific knowledge (created and disseminated through the printed word) of the eighteenth century (2000: 15, 34, 100). This accommodation of the spoken into the printed word was apparently not, however, so easily accepted within the historical disciplines where the oppositions – written word/truth, spoken word/subversion – reinforced a developing hierarchy of knowledge. As we have already seen, John Aubrey, as a boy, 'did ever love to converse with old men, as living histories'. As an adult in the mid-seventeenth century, however, Aubrey noted that such conversations were no longer as popular as they once had been, and he suggested that the spread of literacy in the countryside was responsible for their demise (Woolf, D. 1988: 50). Modern historians concur, and some go on to point out that the Word's silencing of the Voice also meant that *national* histories supplanted *local* traditions (Thomas 1986: 120; Woolf, D. 1988: 48).

3. The Word and the press

Thus the triumph of the Word influenced not only the means through which History could be written but also which histories were deemed important. Tales of local monuments, landscapes and people, some of them surviving through, and being transformed by, Christianisation and Reformation, thus fell in the face of written accounts of matters of national significance. The meaning of monuments, and the validity of stories told about them, diminished as the Word became the vehicle through which the interests of the state were written.

There were, of course, those who rejected the 'truth' of written accounts precisely because of their association with the educated and powerful (see Thomas 1983: 7; and Chapter 4). Oral tradition, by contrast, was 'masterless history', and so became associated with resistance, dissent and rebellion (Woolf, D. 1988: 37; 1991: 188-92). Similarly, Alexandra Walsham notes the use of the spoken word to spread anti-Protestant propaganda (2000: 114). These associations with the socially and ideologically marginalised could only have contributed to the further debasement of the 'authority' of oral traditions among the godly and the powerful – those, in many cases, who wrote the new authorised histories.

Contextualising the Word

The aim of the last two chapters has been to contextualise, and thus to relativise, 'our obsession with the book'. As Donald McKenzie argues, this should be situated 'in the highly relative context of the last few hundred years of European history' (1999: 41). In classical antiquity, both Herodotus and Thucydides regarded oral tradition as the superior source (see below, p. 124 n. 8), and the works of all ancient historians were designed to be read out and heard (Woolf, D. 1986: 185). Similarly, although historians began, from the twelfth century, to prefer the 'longer memory' of written sources, their works were

73

to a large extent constructed on the basis of 'memorised traditions' and on 'lore associated with the places they visited' (Woolf, D. 1988: 28). Even in the early sixteenth century, John Leland sought out oral traditions, recognising that written accounts did not provide a full account of the past (Woolf, D. 1988: 29). Right up to the birth of modernity, the Voice drew upon the 'imaginative memories' of monuments, objects and places to construct the past:

> Ancient stone circles were said to be armies or wedding guests turned into stone. Cromlechs and barrows were the graves of ancient princes or tombs of men slain in great battles …. Curiously shaped rocks were the work of giants or the Devil … or of King Arthur (Thomas 1983: 5; also Woolf, D. 1991).

By the end of the seventeenth century, things were entirely different. The final victory of the concept of *logos* as Truth, the concomitant destruction of the material world of the Catholic past, the supreme faith placed in the written authority of the Ancients (especially Moses), and the power of the printing press, not only contributed to radical transformations in the way the past was perceived and could be written in early modern England, they also played their part in the birth of modernity itself.

Local knowledge, constructed in and through a material world of landscapes and monuments, and played out in the routines and rituals of daily and seasonal life, were some of the victims of that birth. A world of engagement and experience was transformed into one in which its detritus was observed, measured and recorded for inclusion in regional, pan-regional and national histories. Reformation diktats, enclosure agreements and histories told in books separated people from the world of their ancestors, and their imaginative memories withered.

74

3. The Word and the press

In terms of this process of distancing/separation, the fact that Europe was at this time experiencing a 'consumer revolution' is perhaps as significant as any of the factors I have discussed. At the same time as the Word was achieving epistemological primacy and the meaning of the material world was being lost in the destruction of imaginative memory, people in England began, on an unprecedented scale, to acquire and to surround themselves with objects (Styles 2000; Burke 2000: 171). However, changes in production meant that individuals were more removed from a direct engagement with the actual process of *making*, while the penetration of the 'market' into more and more spheres of exchange increased the prevalence of *impersonal* forms of acquisition.[13] The consequence was that, although people lived in a world in which there were more and more objects, they had less engagement with them.[14] This distance/separation, it can be argued, contributed to an inability to see that objects tell stories, that they can and do bear meanings. Many people have commented on the significance of our inhabitation of a world full of words for our valorisation of the text; fewer have commented on the possibility that our alienation from production may have conditioned us to see the artifact as mute (see Hoskins 1998: 192).

I emphasise once again that, despite their institutionalisation in the practice of archaeology and history, the silenced Voice, the mute Artifact, and the all-knowing Word are *recent* phenomena. As we shall see (Chapter 5), some historians and archaeologists now question the ability even of the Word to speak of 'truth', but it is one of the fundamental contentions of this book that we sacrifice any hope of really understanding the past if we impose on it conceptions of the Object, Voice and Word which are of such recent historicity. I would contend that we simply cannot understand any historical past if we 'exalt the primacy of the word to the level of the eternal' and simply assume that the object-world is mute. For most of the historical past we have little hope of directly recovering the words of the Voice, but the techniques and theory of modern archaeology enable us to understand the meanings of Objects. It is only by combining this power of archaeology to discover the meaning of objects *in* the past with an understanding of documents as something other than simply evidence *about* the past that we can come close to reconstructing the means by which society and the self were produced and transformed. In the next chapter I will try to show how this might be done and thus begin the process of piecing together the fragments into which we have shattered the remnants of the past.

4

Objects and texts in context

Not long before, a system of evil signs had been discovered in … [Sumer], that was called *writing*. Almost indistinguishable lines and dots were traced on clay tablets, looking like the marks of crows' feet; apparently these lines and dots had the power to mummify the thoughts of men, just as bodies could be embalmed. And as if that were not quite enough, these tablets were baked in ovens and then sent from one to another as messages (Kadare 1996: 13).

Time had more than one writing-system (Lefebvre 1991: 110).

People without history

The 'democratisation' of archaeological and historical research, from at least the 1960s onwards, found expression in a desire, discovered in the apparent failure of written sources to speak explicitly about the peasantry and other socially marginalised groups, to give voice to the 'people without history' (Deagan 1991; Orser 1996: 160-1). It is my contention, however, that the silencing of the oppressed is not simply a product of their 'absence' from texts (see below, and Chapter 5). Rather they were silenced through the operation of various technologies of oppression which drew upon the resources provided by the material world *and* by the written word. To hear their voices, however faintly, we must abandon our fixation with texts and artifacts simply as *evidence* in the present (although they certainly are that) and consider more carefully how words and things were used, manipulated, and imposed *in the past*.

I will develop these arguments further below, but here I want to suggest that, through the theoretical perspectives we use, we have deprived *all* the peoples of the past of History. Within the 'culture-history' approach to archaeology, archaeologists focused their attention on the relationships between reified cultures and, working within a theoretical perspective which saw culture as essentially conservative, emphasised migration and diffusion as agents of transformation (Jones, S. 1997: 14-26; Shennan 1989; Trigger 1989: 148-206). In these archaeological histories, 'cultures', not people, were the performers on the historical stage; archaeologists typologised and traced the movement of artifacts; people, as the mere bearers of culture, were effectively erased from the historical process.

Within New Archaeology the view that culture was an 'extra-somatic means of adaptation for the human organism' (Binford 1972: 22) resulted in an ultimately conservative view of society in which people reacted, via the objects and institutions they created, to external stimuli in an attempt to return to a pre-existing stable state. Human creativity was reduced to behavioural response in a depersonalised past (Binford 1989: 48; South 1988). In addition, the New Archaeological emphasis on the processes which lay behind and determined 'events' encouraged a tendency to view human action as epiphenomenal. As in Braudellian *Annalisme*, human action, responding to the dictates of underlying (and largely unrecognised) structures and processes, had little place in the making of History.[1] Similarly, the belief that human behaviour in the past was conditioned by a series of universal laws served, through the effective imposition of our present values and *mores*, only to reduce the diversity and difference which existed in the past (Moreland

1997: 168-9). While New Archaeology may initially have been welcomed by the emerging archaeologies of some post-colonial countries in their efforts to rewrite imperialist and oppressing histories (see Chapter 1), its ultimate effect was to deny History to all.

Similarly, within structuralist archaeologies humans are inherently passive, responding only to stimuli from largely subconscious or unconscious structures which act 'behind their backs' (Geertz 1993c: 356-7; Hall 2000: 44, 48-52; Johnson 1999: 90-2). The same is true of archaeological histories based on an orthodox reading of Marx, in which the superfluity of human endeavour in effecting change is made clear by assigning causal primacy in historical directionality to contradictions between the (impersonal) forces and relations of production (for more nuanced readings, see some of the papers in Spriggs 1984).

Finally, there are those histories which claim to be written from an atheoretical, 'common sense', point of view. The claim here is that no theory is necessary; words and objects from the past, as facts, speak for themselves. In fact, 'common sense history' simply overwrites the past and recreates it in our own likeness; human action in the past is rendered meaningless other than in *our* terms (see Bloch 1953: 80; Moreland 1998: 88-9; Moreland 2000).

Within these perspectives humans are the bearers and victims of cultural projects (sometimes ours); their puny actions are meaningless in the face of the power of forces of which they are unaware. Objects and texts are seen simply as *evidence* for the operation of process and structure in the past, or as a passive *reflection* of group identities which had primordial biological roots. In essence, the prime focus is on the evidential value of objects and texts in the *present*, rather than their power *in the past*. It is as if people in the past did not engage in any meaningful way with the objects and texts they created. Instead

79

these are only activated in the service of archaeologists and historians in the present.

Significant possessions

The reality is that people in the past, as in the present, made and manipulated objects (and texts) as projections of their views about themselves and their place in the world. Products of human creativity and invention were not simply essentialist reflections of an inner (given) reality. Rather, they were *actively* used in the production and transformation of identities; they were used in the projection of, and in resistance to, power; and they were used to create meaning in, and to structure, the routines of everyday life. The sword that Giselpert seized from the tomb of Alboin in the eighth century was not simply a *reflection* of his power; it was activated in its construction and reproduction (see Chapter 2, and Geary 1994b). The iconoclasts who destroyed the Bradbourne cross (Fig. 6) in the late sixteenth or early seventeenth century did so precisely because they were only too aware of its meaning to the parishioners, of their ability to 'read' it, and of its role in structuring and reproducing the ritual life of the parish (Moreland 1999b). The gardens laid out by the elites of eighteenth-century America were not simply islands of 'domesticated nature' in a sea of wilderness, nor were they merely a reflection of elite power. Constructed by elites, these gardens in turn contributed to the construction of their power and identity (see Leone 1988a, 1988b; and below, Chapter 5).

Nor is meaning ascribed to, and derived from, elite or ritual objects alone. Rather, as Janet Hoskins argues, the imagination works on all kinds of objects 'to turn commodities, gifts, or ordinary utilitarian tools into sometimes very significant possessions, which draw their power from biographical experiences and the stories told about these' (1998: 196; also above, p. 39).

4. Objects and texts in context

The disengagement of the individual from the material world evident in so much archaeological writing is thrown into sharp relief by anthropological observations (such as those of Hoskins) of a deep and profound intimacy between people and the objects they make and possess (also Remensnyder 1996).

Some might counter that although objects, even utilitarian ones, *were* assigned meaning in the past, we are in no position to reconstruct them. As I suggested above, through the use of 'inappropriate' methodologies we have to some extent placed ourselves in this position.[2] Changing our perspectives on the knowledgeability and creativity of people in the past might allow us to hear them more clearly.

Anthony Giddens' theory of structuration, and its appropriation within what has become known as 'post-processual' archaeology, provides us with just such an alternative perspective.[3] Giddens proposed that societal structures should be seen as both the product of human action in the past and the field in which human action takes places in the present (Giddens 1979: 69; also Giddens 1981: 54; Barrett 1988). People are born into communities which are structured through knowledge, rules and practices – the accumulated product of past human action. People acquire a kind of 'habitual knowledge' about how their world works through the daily practice of living within it. This is complemented by a more *discursive knowledge*, a product of the fact that 'all social actors, no matter how lowly, have some degree of penetration of the social forms which oppress them' (Giddens 1979: 72). This acknowledgement of human knowledgeability about their own condition leads to the possibility of the 'reordering or transformation of structures because meanings and principles of conduct are re-evaluated in practice' (Shanks and Tilley 1987: 72).

The application of structuration theory within archaeology has dramatically altered our perception of material culture. If we see people in the past as knowledgeable about the structures

81

within which they lived, and as capable of taking action in attempts to reproduce or transform those structures, then we begin to see the remains of their past as *creations* produced in pursuit of these ends. Material culture becomes both the product of actions which are articulated through social relationships and, at the same time, one of the means through which social relationships are constructed, produced and transformed. Material culture ceases to be a *passive* element in social practice and a *passive* reflection of identity and becomes an *active* intervention in the production of community and self. Henrietta Moore summarises the position: 'material culture embodies meaning, it is the product of meaningful action, and it is involved in the reproduction of meaningful action in determinate social and historical contexts' (Moore 1990: 112; also Moreland 1991a: 20-1; 1998: 101-2). However, the question of whether we can now read such meanings remains.

I would argue that we can come to an 'evaluated approximation to understanding' (Hodder 1986: 124) by situating a detailed examination of the material remains of the past within a theoretical perspective which sees them as something more than reflections of identity or adaptive responses. Ian Hodder refers to this as 'contextual archaeology', and describes it as the 'interweaving, or connecting, of things in their historical particularity' (1986: 119). The main task of the archaeologist is to situate an artifact or group of artifacts within its contemporary context by seeking out the range of similarities and differences it shares with other artifacts or groups. Meaning is not inherent in any particular object of material culture but derives from its relationships with other objects. Just as medieval churchmen tried to use written inscriptions to control the 'luxuriant polysemy' of the material world (above, p. 49), so the possible readings of objects in the past was similarly constrained by their relationship with other objects – by their context.

It is important to recognise that an artifact's context spans a range of spatial and temporal scales. Our ability to reconstruct the meaning of the seventh-century burials in the prehistoric mound at Wigber Low (Fig. 3), for example, is dependent not only on the discovery of datable weapons and jewellery in the physical context of this particular Bronze Age barrow. Our knowledge of similar burials throughout the lands settled by the Anglo-Saxons, of the importance of tombs and the dead in Germanic ideology, and of the cross-cultural importance of the ancestors in influencing the world of the living are all elements in the construction of the context which allows us to understand the meaning attached to this act by those who stood on this hilltop hundreds of years ago (see Collis 1983; Geary 1994b; Williams 1998).

Contextual archaeology demands a close and detailed engagement with data, and should result in the production of histories with affinities to the kind of thick description advocated by Clifford Geertz and the 'microhistories' of recent historical scholarship (Geertz 1993d; Egmond and Mason 1997). As Geertz puts it, 'the aim is to draw large conclusions from small, but very densely textured facts' (1993d: 28). Contextual archaeology also demands that we use *all* the data we have available from the past. This means that 'it no longer becomes possible to study one arbitrarily defined aspect of the data on its own' (Hodder 1986: 139) – such as texts *or* objects. For if it is the case that material culture should be seen as a product of human creativity, as an active intervention in the social production of reality, then it must follow that this applies to *all* human creations – including written sources (see Moreland 1991a: 20-1).

The word 'context' derives from the Latin *contexere* meaning to weave, join together, or connect (Hodder 1986: 119). Archaeologists must recognise that people in the historical past wove or constructed their identities, not just from the objects they created, possessed and lived within, but through texts as well

(Moreland 1998: 90-5).[4] As products of human creativity, they too were created and distributed within social relationships, and were crucial weapons in attempts to reproduce or transform them. As such, the 'silent majority', although illiterate, were deeply entangled in the webs created by writing. Equally, however, historians must recognise that their exclusive focus on the written sources provides them with access to only one thread in the fabric of human identity – hardly a reliable basis for the reconstruction of the whole.

Finally, we should note that one of the consequences of seeing both objects and texts as human *creations* is to distance the latter from language and so remove what is left of its 'primordial' essence.[5] Walter Ong argues that writing is no 'mere accessory or appendage to oral speech', but a *technology* which 'moves speech drastically from the oral-aural or voice-ear world to a sensory world, that of vision' (Ong 1986: 35; also Woolf, D. 1986; and above, Chapter 3). We can connect this with Jack Goody's observation that 'speech is associated with the left side [of the brain] and visio-spatial activity (e.g. writing) with the right' (Goody 1977: 123). Writing and objects, as creations, thus have much more in common than many historians and archaeologists allow. Persisting in fragmenting the past on the basis of a difference between them, we not only unpick the weave through which people constructed themselves in the past, we also separate what is in our own brain.

The 'literacy thesis'

As I discussed at some length in Chapters 2 and 3, during the European middle ages (and elsewhere, see p. 45), the power of writing was intimately linked with, and, to some extent derived, from its association with the supernatural and with 'truth'. The 'power of the word', however, did not reside solely in its links with the divine. Jack Goody and Walter Ong (among others) have argued that writing should be seen as a *technology* with efficacy, not only in the production and transformation of social relations, but also in altering the very way we think (Goody 1968, 1977, 1986; Ong 1986; Olson 1994). In what has become known as the 'literacy thesis', they have argued that writing, as a new means of communication, transformed the 'nature of cognitive processes' (Goody 1977: 18, 36; Ong 1986: 34).

The transformational powers of writing, Goody suggests, derive from the fact that it,

> and more especially alphabetic literacy, made it possible to scrutinise discourse in a different kind of way by giving oral communication a semi-permanent form; this scrutiny favoured the increase in scope of critical activity, and hence of rationality, scepticism, and logic (1977: 37; also Herrenschmidt 2000).

Similarly, Walter Ong argues that writing separated logic from rhetoric, and he asserts that 'all formal logic in the world, down to that used for computers, stems from the ancient Greeks' (1986: 40-1).

Within the 'literacy thesis', therefore, writing is never a 'neutral' means of recording events, perceptions and ideas. Through its capacity to 'materialise' speech, to open it up to inspection, scrutiny and storage, writing is, rather, a technology instrumental in the transformation (some would say creation) of humanity. This view has had some impact on perceptions of the significance of texts in the past. Jean Bottéro begins his study of ancient Sumerian sources from the premise that 'writing revolutionised human thought' (2000: 20). Similarly, Clarisse Herrenschmidt has argued that writing dramatically altered 'the form in which humans beings were to think the world' (2000: 110), and Charles Briggs has noted the argument

85

of some medievalists that innovations in textual production and usage 'caused profound changes in the thought of those associated with them' (2000: 415-16; also Burke 2000: 11, 51).

In recent years, however, the literacy thesis has been subjected to sustained critique. Critics have argued, for example, that Ong and Goody draw too sharp a distinction between oral ('traditional/conservative') and literate ('modern/progressive') societies. This is an element in a wider critique of assumptions about progress and 'the superiority of Western rationality and literacy' inherent in the thesis (Collins 1995: 80). Further, John Halverson has sought to undermine it by showing that many of the processes and skills thought to be a product of writing are in fact present in oral communities; scrutiny can take place within orality. He notes that 'the critical comparison of different stories is a commonplace of everyday oral life' (1992: 310), and concludes that 'there are no implications in any of this for distinctive "cognitive structures and processes" ' (1992: 306).[6]

Critics have also pointed to the tendency of proponents to see writing as a 'thing-in-itself, as an autonomous technology', thereby ignoring its embeddedness, 'its nature and meaning shaped by, rather than determinate of, broad cultural-historical frameworks and specific historical practices' (Collins 1995: 78). Halverson concludes that 'the *medium* of communication ... has no *intrinsic* significance in the communication of ideas or the development of logical thought processes' (1992: 314).

The proponents of the literacy thesis have, in fact, accepted the force of some of the arguments presented against them. Thus Goody and Ong have strenuously denied that they see writing as a disembedded technology, exercising its force regardless of historical context (Goody 1986: xv-xvi; Ong 1986: 35). Equally, we might argue that the critics have overstated their case. It is certainly noteworthy that people in the past themselves seem to have been aware that written accounts offered the potential for scrutiny, reflection and scepticism.

86

Thus, in 1637, 'Archbishop Laud ... speaking ... in the Star Chamber ... asserted that what was written could be reflected upon, analysed and criticised, unlike the spoken word' (Woolf, D. 1986: 176), while Carlo Ginzburg refers to the 'relativistic shock' suffered by the sixteenth-century miller Domenico Scandella (Menocchio) when he read the *Travels* of Sir John Mandeville (Ginzburg 1982: 44-5).

There was also an awareness (*contra* Halverson 1992: 314) that the medium of communication did have a significant impact on the communication of ideas. The appropriation of writing by some of the participants in the Peasants' Revolt in England in 1381 was itself a message to their oppressors (Justice 1994: 25; also below, p. 93). In 1707 John Locke published an essay in which he considered the significance of the standard practice of presenting Biblical narrative in short verses. He argued that this allowed people to take the 'loose Sentences, and Scripture crumbled into Verses' as distinct aphorisms for use in their social and political struggles, and to prevent this he contended that the Bible should be printed, 'as the several Parts of it were Writ', in 'continued Discourses' (cited in McKenzie 1999: 56). Here too, the medium affected the message.

None of this entails an acceptance that writing was *the* prime architect in the construction of rationality, logic etc., and here the proponents of the literacy thesis are certainly guilty of privileging western forms of thought. It must also be remembered, however, that such assertions are only one element in the literacy thesis. Embedded within this are arguments for the *social and political power* of writing (see even Halverson 1992: 316).

The power of the Word

In recent years there has been a shift, at least partially as a result of the kind of critiques referred to above, away from 'universalist' perceptions of writing to a new awareness of the historical specificity and embeddedness of the practice, and of its connection with power (see Collins 1995: 75-6). Brinkley Messick sums up these new directions in his 'view of writing that stresses its cultural and historical variability, and its implications in terms of relations of domination rather than its neutrality or transparency as a medium' (1993: 2).

The multiplicity of literacies is in fact acknowledged in the literacy thesis. Thus, in one of his earliest works on the subject, Goody argued that 'writing is not a monolithic entity ... its potentialities depend upon the kind of system that obtains in any particular society' (1968: 3; also 1977: 147). Similarly, his observation that 'the skill of writing is a scarce resource' (1968: 19) demonstrates his understanding that such literacies were intimately entangled with structures of power. Writing, in fact, can be seen as a *technology of power*, used and manipulated in different ways at different times depending on the specific historical context, but always with profound effects on the way people in the past (even the illiterate) lived their lives.

Scholars from a range of disciplines have noted the intimacy of the association between writing and power. It is perhaps most forcefully expressed in Lévi-Strauss' argument that writing 'seems to have favoured the exploitation of human beings rather than their enlightenment. The primary function of written communication is to facilitate slavery' (1989: 392-3; also Giddens 1981: 169-70; 1979: 95). Foucault has suggested that 'in this slender technique [i.e. writing] are to be found a whole domain of knowledge, a whole type of power' (1979: 185). Discussing Sumerian texts, Clarisse Herrenschmidt argues that

> insofar as a cylinder seal impression on a bulla was the signature of a functionary, indicating an administrative action and therefore, in the event, *a repression*, it is possible to say that people began to write because *written*

accounts maintained social order (2000: 79, emphasis added).

The fourteenth-century English peasant insurgents who communicated some of their demands in writing did so because they understood that in their world 'authority claimed without writing would be no authority at all' (Justice 1994: 127; also Briggs 2000: 418; Thomas 1986: 120).[7]

As Jack Goody pointed out, writing in most historical societies was *socially restricted* (above, p. 88, and Goody 1968: 11-20); it was usually controlled and exercised by secular and ecclesiastical elites, or scribes in their employ. As we have already seen in Chapter 2, literacy in medieval Europe could hardly be called universal, and was very directly associated with secular and (especially) ecclesiastical elites. In Mesoamerica, 'reading and writing skills [were] restricted to a small segment of society', and this elite monopoly of writing meant that they 'controlled both the content of the message and one of its major vehicles' (Marcus 1992: 27, 11).[8] Writing was clearly a technology whose potential was recognised and appreciated by those whose dominance within society provided them with the means to restrict access to it. In worlds where the text could '*become* the word of god' (Beard 1991: 50), and where it was believed that 'whatever was inscribed with writing would be eternally alive' (Marcus 1992: 13), it was too powerful a tool to place in the hands of the masses. But, as I have argued, its real potential owed as much to the fact that it is a product of human creativity – a technology.

At the beginning of the seventh century, the early Christian theologian Isidore of Seville wrote that such is the power of 'letters' that 'they speak to us without voice the discourse of the absent' (cited in Gellrich 1985: 6). Isidore was referring to the 'preservative potentiality of writing' – one of the central elements in construction of the 'literacy thesis' which even its critics admit survives their assaults (Halverson 1992: 316). Jack Goody claims that perhaps the most significant feature of writing is that it enables 'speech [to] ... be *transmitted over space and preserved over time* .... The range of human intercourse can now be greatly extended both in time and space' (1968: 1-2, emphasis added; also Ong 1986). Thoughts and deeds, rights and duties, could now be 'permanently' recorded, and communicated to the future and to those geographically removed from the writer. The creation of such records meant that 'the capacity of the memory store could be increased so that more transactions could be kept track of ... at any one time' (Goody 1986: 78; Bottéro 2000: 19-20).

These records were not neutral and dispassionate observations; they were not simply records. They were produced and disseminated in and through a medium controlled by elites, and were constructed to service their desires. They offered elites the capacity to generate (and store) more knowledge about, and thus the ability to exercise more control over, their subjects. So writing could be used to record taxation and to create a list of those liable to pay taxes – the basis of any census (Goody 1986: 63). With this recording of liabilities and names went increased control over both people and the product of their labour.

Interestingly, it seems that the 'surveillance' possibilities offered by the written word were appreciated from the beginning. In Mesopotamia, in the fourth and third millennia BC, the earliest written accounts emerged as part of a 'book-keeping system: receipts, lists of expenses, of animals, of all kinds of goods, or of raw materials' (Nissen 1986: 324; also Giddens 1981: 95; Goody 1977: 82). Similarly, the Linear B archives from the Mycenaean palaces of late Bronze Age Greece comprised 'inventories of palatial resources ... and records of the movement of these resources to, from and within the palatial system' (Halstead 1992: 59). The penetration of Roman bureaucracy into, for example, the village of Karanis in Egypt effectively monitored the residents' production and consumption of beer, grain, cloth etc., and ensured that they paid the appropriate taxes on each (Hopkins 1991: 139).

In each case, the powerful monitored and recorded the activities of the powerless. Writing provided a fixed and 'objective' account of the land, labour and resources owed to the former by the latter. It (at least potentially) provided elites with the possibility of reflexively monitoring 'economic' strategies with a view to increasing their share of productive resources, and thus their power. It created a record whose permanence only served to highlight the 'fragility of memory', and whose objectivity would countenance no appeal to memories of tradition.[9] Possession of, or control over, such an unimpeachable and unforgetful witness was both an instrument in, and a sign of, elite power. Further, these 'administrative' documents, in the very act of recording, fixing and defining their subjects in the text, served to fix and define their place in the world. In eleventh-century England people linked William the Conqueror's 'Domesday' survey of 'every ox, cow or pig in the land' with the 'book of Life' which would be opened at the Last Judgement – in both, they were named, assessed and consigned to their fate (Camille 1985a: 36; Clanchy 1993: 140). Finally, and perhaps most dramatically, the textual indexing techniques devised by medieval churchmen formed the basis for the 'technology of documentation' used to interrogate, classify and condemn to death the 'heretics' of Christian Europe (Briggs 2000: 416; more generally, see Foucault 1979: 189-92).

Writing was not, of course, confined to recording the workings of bureaucracy in early historic societies, but affected all aspects of life. The texts of the medieval and early modern church were one element in the structuring of the daily and seasonal rituals through which people expressed their relationship with the supernatural (Duffy 1992; also above, Chapter 2). Similarly, Mary Beard argues that, during the late Roman republic, the use of writing as a medium of communication with the supernatural, and as a means of structuring the ritual cycle, 'fundamentally affect[ed] the whole character of Roman religious organisation' and ultimately what it meant to be Roman (Beard 1991: 56, 54; also Beard 1987; Salzman 1990). Writing did not just record; it also structured social practice. Furthermore, elite control over the production of, and access to, the liturgical texts, histories and calendars which represented and structured the ritual year, contributed to the impression that *they* were responsible for the coherency embedded within such texts. They were the powerful ones who, in communion with the gods, provided the world with order and meaning.[10]

James Collins has argued that 'identities are not just shaped but are radically constituted by the literate vs. illiterate dichotomy' (1995: 83). Writing was an element in the constitution of elite identity. In tenth-century Byzantium, letters were written in an obscure literary style which became 'a badge of membership of an elite club' (Mullett 1990: 179);[11] while in an earlier Roman world a common 'literary culture ... reinforced the unification of the political elite across the Mediterranean basin' (Hopkins 1991: 142-3; see also Burke 2000: 19, 57 for the early modern 'Republic of Letters'). The restricted nature of literacy, the arenas in which it was deployed, and its role in the definition of one's place in a 'field of power', all serve to reinforce our impression of the written word as a technology of oppression.

There is, however, a danger of presenting a one-dimensional picture of the efficacy of writing in historic societies. By focusing on writing in this section, I run the risk of appearing to offer it as *the* principal form of discourse, as *the* only technology of oppression. Writing *was* important for all the reasons outlined above, but, as I have tried to emphasise throughout this book, we have to consider its efficacy in the context of other discourses in particular historical circumstances. As I have argued above and elsewhere (Moreland 1998), people in the past wove their identities from the threads provided by written, spoken *and* material discourses. This book is written in response to our unpicking of these threads in the present fragmentation of the disciplines which study the historical past, and to remind those working in historic periods that written accounts are so much more than evidence *about* the past. However, we must always remember, with Brinkley Messick, that 'textual domination is a partial phenomenon, one that intersects in each historical instance with other dimensions of authority and with the relations of a specific mode of production' (1993: 1).

There is also a danger of over-emphasising elite hegemony over writing. People in the past had some comprehension of the technologies which oppressed them, and occasionally we see them grasping and using these in pursuit of *their* ends. I have already referred to the use of writing by some of the insurgents in the Peasants' Revolt of 1381 (above, p. 87). These letters communicated their demands to their oppressors, and they show the oppressed learning 'the language of the conquerors in order to borrow the conqueror's power, and to protect themselves from exploitation' (Hopkins 1991: 137). However, they (like written sources in the present) did more than communicate information. They staked a claim to power and threatened the identity of those who believed they controlled writing. As Steven Justice argues, 'in asserting that literacy existed where it did not belong, they drew the class line, the line that separated the exploited from the exploiters, at exactly the point where writing was controlled' (1994: 192).

Like others who occasionally survive the deliberate amnesia which clouds official accounts, these English peasants also appropriated the power of the word by destroying it. Wherever rebellion broke out, the peasants systematically sought out and destroyed 'the artificial memory that sustained the mechanisms of extraction' (Justice 1994: 155; also Briggs 2000: 418; Burke 2000: 138). Importantly for the argument I have been trying to create in this book, these fourteenth-century insurgents did not construct their community and identity only through and against written texts. In an illuminating incident, they broke into the monastery of St Albans and seized the handmills which, as a symbol of the monastery's control over milling, had been taken from them, broken and inserted into the parlour floor 'as a document and memorial (*in munimentum et memoriam*)' of the dispute (Justice 1994: 168). The rebels too read this material 'document', but they read it differently, and then destroyed it just as they had the written kind.[12]

Entangled with words and things

Despite these appropriations of the potency of writing, it remains the case that most people in the past were denied access to its form and excluded from its content. For many archaeologists, this is taken to mean that the written sources tell us primarily about the lives and worldview of elites, have little to say about the vast majority of the population, and not much more about 'the economy' and everyday life. This 'absence' in the written sources is then taken as providing a field within which archaeology can operate (see Chapter 1). The oppressed may not normally have written texts, and the oppressors may not have written about their 'victims' often enough to satisfy our craving for the certainty of the Word, but it is one of the main contentions of this book that we make a gross error when we mistake an (apparent) absence in written sources in the present for the lack of any engagement in the past.

As I have outlined above, such was the 'power of the word' in the past that it fundamentally altered the social relationships within which *all* people lived (Austin 1990: 29-30). Ancient authors may not have written frequently and explicitly about production, exchange and the 'everyday' (cleverly leaving a space in the 'house of history' for the lowly archaeologist). This

does not, however, leave a text-free zone within which archaeology can work its practice without fear of contradiction from
history (see Chapter 1), for, as we have just seen, many of the
written accounts we possess – even some of the earliest – were
dedicated to administration and control in this arena of human
activity. This deployment of writing entangled everyone in its
web. Just as elites were 'actors in the public transcripts of
domination' they constructed (Hall 2000: 31), so the rest of the
people were (to some extent at least) 'victims' of such texts (see,
for example, Baines 1983: 586). However, writing did more than
contribute to economic exploitation. Even here, on the bottom
rung of the Hawkesian ladder, people were monitored, controlled and defined by the power of the word. They constructed their
identities through and in opposition to its demands. Even here,
writing was a thread in the fabric of identity. The silent majority are not just absent from the written accounts; the texts were
operational in 'silencing the world of the dominated' (Messick
1993: 5).

Just as we must avoid the trap of assuming that writing did
not penetrate to the bottom of the Hawkesian ladder, so we
must be equally wary of supposing that, because elites controlled access to the supernatural through the written word, it did
not touch the lives of the illiterate. Here too, in the realm of
belief and ideology, everyone was entangled in the web of the
Word. In the Roman world, Mary Beard argues, the existence
of 'written representations of the religious "system" ... determined the nature of ... religious experience', even for the
completely illiterate (1991: 58). More generally, Keith Hopkins
suggests that, despite the fact that few could read and write,

> the whole experience of living in the Roman empire, of
> being ruled by Romans, was overdetermined by the exist-
> ence of texts. ... The mass of literates, the density of their
> communications, and the volumes of their stored knowl-

95

edge, significantly altered the experience of living in the Roman empire (1991: 144).

The same could probably be said of most societies in the historic past.

As I have stated before, and as I must emphasise again, this discussion of the power of the word should not be taken to mean that I believe that it was *the* prime discourse, *the* principal technology of oppression, in the past. As I argued in Chapter 3, it was only in recent times that the Word eclipsed the Object and reduced the Voice to a whisper. The point of this discussion has been to emphasise that just as the material world was more than adaptive response or a 'reflection' of identity, so the written word was more than a 'neutral' recording system. Both were *active*, or activated, in social practice, in the construction of identity, in the production and transformation of social relations, and in the exercise of (and resistance to) power.

People in the past constructed their identities through an engagement with memory, texts and the material world (Moreland 1998). Historians who focus only on the *content* of texts weave for these people a warped identity from a very denuded thread. Archaeologists are equally guilty. In ignoring the engagement between texts and the 'people without history', they deny themselves the possibility of fully understanding the mechanisms through which the latter were exploited. In disregarding the palaces and castles of the elite in a misguided search for the everyday life of the 'people without history', they ignore the fact that the latter contributed, through their oppression, to the construction and reproduction of the former, and confronted them every day as a visible reminder of exploitation (see Austin 1998). The very monumentality of the castle, the stridency of its claims to domination, contains an awareness of resistance to those claims and bears the 'impress of the unseen but constantly present subaltern voice' (Hall 2000: 39; also Hall 1992: 392).[13]

Oppressor and oppressed were entangled in webs spun through texts and objects. We will never understand their pasts if we unpick this weave and see the separate threads simply as evidence *about* the past. If we are fully to understand the historical past, we must seek out the details of the way in which people, in historically specific contexts, used, manipulated and confronted both texts and objects. We have to reconstruct the details of their entanglement with words and things, and write the kind of 'thick descriptions' which allow the variety and ingenuity of human creativity, and the difference of the past, to shine through. Only an explicitly theoretical understanding of what historical archaeology is will allow us to do this; a failure to theorise (or the use of 'inappropriate' theories) makes it impossible to understand the past in anything like its own terms.

5

What is historical archaeology?

The literacy of the people it studies is what sets historical archaeology apart from prehistory (Deetz 1977: 7).

In America ... a popular definition of historical archaeology is the archaeology of the spread of European culture throughout the world since the fifteenth century and its impact on indigenous peoples (Deetz 1977: 5).

An archaeology of the modern world?

In recent years, archaeologists working on the medieval and post-medieval periods in Britain have bemoaned the poverty of theory within their fields (for example, Moreland 1991a; Tarlow 1999). It is argued that the failure to recognise the imperative of taking an explicitly theoretical approach in historic periods stems from the apparent certitude offered by the presence of the written word (Arnold 1986: 36; Austin 1990: 31), or from the implicit understanding that we are dealing with people already familiar to us due to their proximity in time and their portrayal in histories, novels and drama (Orser 1996: 15; Tarlow 1999: 263). One response to this 'poverty of theory' in British historical archaeologies has been to look for inspiration in what is

perceived as a more fully developed American historical archaeology (for example, West 1999: 2; Tarlow 1999: 271).[1]

Given the *reality* of atheoretical (and even anti-theoretical)
historical archaeologies in Britain (and in much of the rest
of Europe), it is immediately understandable why the
trans-Atlantic prospect looks so much rosier – especially
for post-medieval archaeologists. American historical archaeology focuses on much the same time period as the latter, and
it appears to do so using a theoretical perspective which acknowledges the efficacy of the material world in social practice.
The work of Mark Leone *et al.* at Annapolis, Maryland, gives
some flavour of the kind of approach deemed enviable by post-
medieval archaeologists in Britain.

The research of Leone, and of others working in the eastern United States, has been dedicated to showing how new
principles of order and control emerged in the context of
growing social and economic divisions, and in the face of the
threat posed by the actions of the British government to the
power and autonomy of newly emergent elites in the eighteenth century (Leone 1984; 1988a). It is argued that these
new principles of order, symmetry, segmentation, stand-
ardisation and discipline (known as the 'Georgian Order') are
not simply reflected in the material culture of the period, but
that the latter served to inculcate the new worldview and
ultimately to bolster the power and authority of elites
(Johnson 1996: 202-4).

In one of the most famous studies in American historical
archaeology, Mark Leone argued that in the 1760s William
Paca, one of the signatories of the Declaration of Independence,
created a garden in Annapolis which, through its imposition of
order, segmentation and the rules of perspective on the world of
nature, and through the knowledge it displayed about the
workings of nature and of the past, sent a powerful message to

his contemporaries (Leone 1988a: 242). It was a demonstration that he, and people like him, commanded the world,

> for by walking in it, building it, looking at it, admiring and discussing it, ... its contemporaries could take themselves and their position as granted and convince others that the way things are is the way they always had been and should remain (Leone 1984: 34).[2]

Leone goes on to argue that such attempts to naturalise the 'hierarchical conditions of social life' in landscape architecture were later replaced by more overt political action, culminating in the Declaration of Independence (1988a: 256). Gardens and houses were not, however, the only objects to create and display the message of the new order. It is no coincidence, he implies, that clocks, watches and scientific instruments appeared in Annapolis just when the social order was experiencing dramatic change. Not only were these 'items of precision' used to 'observe, study, order, and rationalise natural phenomena', but the

> rules, etiquette, regulations and routines it took to use them introduced mechanical or cultural divisions into every-day life and modelled daily life's activities on the mechanically precise rules of the clockwork universe (1988a: 242).

In conventional archaeological analyses, these instruments would be seen as *passively* reflecting the power and status of their owners (Leone 1988a: 241). Leone, however, demands that we recognise their *active* contribution to the maintenance of elite power. At a time when increasing wealth differentials within the city were contributing to social stress, these measuring devices served in the acquisition of knowledge *about* nature, in order to demonstrate Man's mastery *over* it and, by implica-

Fig. 7. Hans Holbein the Younger (1497/8-1543), *The Ambassadors*, 1533 (photo: © The National Gallery, London)

tion, over human society.[3] As Martin Hall notes, the significance of these instruments in the emerging new world order is manifest in their conspicuous display in Holbein's *The Ambassadors* (Hall 2000: 52). However, his failure to observe, or at least to comment on, the range of 'written objects' also on display in this painting can be taken as symptomatic of the failure of historical archaeology to recognise the efficacy of the written word in the past (Fig. 7).

Leone's work not only puts archaeology at the forefront of

101

historical interpretations in the present, it also recognises the efficacy of objects in the production and reproduction of social relationships in the past. This is a far cry from European historical archaeologies which, despite the exhortations of a few to implement the programmatic of New Archaeology or to exploit the potential of post-processual approaches (Hodges 1982; Moreland 1991a), remain largely the preserve of culture history or 'commonsense' (see Chapter 1). It is my contention, however, that as a model for how historical archaeology should be done, the 'American version' does not go far enough, and that, in the claims of some of its exponents for what historical archaeology is, it goes too far.

Despite its apparent theoretical sophistication, American historical archaeology in fact shares many of the same failings as historical archaeologies across the world (see Chapter 1). Of these, the most significant are an undue respect for, and (paradoxically) a failure to appreciate the full potential of, written sources. In some cases, it appears that the material world is still only knowable in terms of written accounts (for example, Deagan 1991: 103). Interestingly, there are indications that Mark Leone, despite the efficacy he acknowledges for artifacts in the past, sees them as subordinate when it comes to writing histories in the present. Thus he contends that, since texts and artifacts were not made and used by the same people,[4] we should see them as 'different and unidentical phenomena'. While both belong to the past (both are dead), the written account 'is more lively than the archaeological record', it is 'more articulated and thus has greater integrity', and (crucially) 'it is also likely to contain the behaviour and structure behind the parts, rules and divisions, which gives meaning to the whole' (1988b: 33; also Leone and Crosby 1987: 409). Archaeological patterns are thus given meaning through the content of written sources. The artifact, if not entirely mute, can only speak through the text. Archaeology remains subservient to, and parasitic upon, history.

There is also a countervailing, and perhaps more pervasive, tendency within this historical archaeology to see written accounts as biased, and as incapable of providing us with insights into the 'reality' of the historical past. The archaeological record, by contrast, because it was not 'consciously' produced, permits the possibility of such insights (Deagan 1991: 103; Deetz 1991: 6; Orser and Fagan 1995: 17). Archaeology does not, however, recover an 'unconscious', 'unintentional' (and therefore supposedly objective) record of and from the past. What we are really interested in are the ways in which meanings were read from and into even everyday, 'utilitarian' objects to make them 'significant possessions'. All objects are conscious productions, and all were implicated in the mundane and extraordinary events of social practice. Further, if we are to fully understand the historical past we cannot afford to ignore the explicit ('conscious', 'intentional') material expressions of power and status (Moreland 1991a; and above, pp. 96-7). Mosaics, statuary, mansions and castles are as much material remains from the past as are the middens, wells and house foundations of the poor. They are the product of exploitation, and in ignoring them we blithely pass over a manifestation of elite power and make all the mistakes of writing history 'with the politics left out' (G.M. Trevelyan, cited in Evans 1997: 166).

This (fundamentally flawed) perception of the archaeological record as somehow especially predisposed to tell us about the poor has contributed to the constant refrain of American historical archaeologists that they are in a *unique* and privileged position to restore the lost voices of the 'people without history'.[5] Charles Orser, for example, claims that archaeologists 'make visible the runaway slaves and the rural peasants', and that it is 'the rightful destiny' of historical archaeology to give 'voice to the otherwise voiceless' (1996: 178-9; also Hall 1993: 186; Leone

103

1995: 251; Orser and Fagan 1995: 20).[6] What they fail to consider, of course, is the role of writing as a technology which contributed to the oppression and 'silence' of the 'voiceless'.

It is given *some* consideration in the best work in the field. Mark Leone, for example, tells us that 'reading and listening also played a part in the spread of the new way of thinking and doing things' in eighteenth-century Annapolis (1988a: 247), but in his 'archaeology of capitalism', which draws explicitly on Foucault who saw writing as a crucial element in disciplinary regimes, writing is considered only once (and then only indirectly) (Leone 1995: 260; Foucault 1979: 189-92). Similarly, in his consideration of the Georgian order, we hear little about how writing was used in the actual process of recording, understanding, disseminating and displaying the new knowledge which made elites a class apart. Their observations of nature were based on principles derived from books, were recorded in texts, and compared with other texts. These lists of observations could also be seen as evidence that they had privileged access to the workings of an 'orderly' nature; that they understood the laws behind that order and were therefore in a supreme position to 'order' society as well (for thoughts along these lines, see Collins 1995: 84; Goody 1977: 50-1). Likewise, although Charles Orser tells us that the peasants of Gorttose, in Ireland, have been largely forgotten because the landowners produced the estate's documentation (1996: 97), he never considers that this 'judgement of historical silence' was in some measure effected through these written records. Interestingly, this is something emphasised by *historians* working in the same region. Robert Scully, for example, notes that 'the townland did not expose its mind to the record-keepers willingly. As part of the "hidden Ireland" ... it was an axiom of survival to evade that surveillance by all means possible' (1995: 4). American historical archaeologists seem prepared to acknowledge the efficacy in the past of every cultural manifestation, apart from the one which defines their discipline.

This takes us back to re-consider the claim of (especially) American historical archaeology that it is in a *unique* position to write the histories of the forgotten. Archaeology can indeed uncover the remains of the oppressed and of those who evaded the record-keepers. However, it is also true that these 'hidden voices' usually remain 'frustratingly elusive' (Hall 2000: 19). Moreover, as I intimated above (p. 104), historians have long directed their energies at reading the 'voiceless' from the written sources, and have, for example, discovered in the probate records of nineteenth-century South Africa a 'reality' of female authority and influence which contradicts accounts of their subordination presented in 'public transcripts' (Hall 2000: 32).

What we have to recognise, as many American historical archaeologists appear not to have done, is that their 'speciality' emerged out of the same context as that which brought a new generation of 'outsiders' into the historical profession – women, blacks, immigrants (the descendents of the voiceless) seeking out the voices of their people. They asked new questions of old texts and examined texts which had been deemed 'useless' for the task of writing of the manifest destiny of the United States. In so doing they made the inarticulate speak, and resurrected the memory of people ignored in the standard white, male, Protestant dominated accounts (Appleby, Hunt and Jacob 1994: 146-7).[7] Their efforts are largely undone, the historically silenced are again rendered mute, by those who dismiss the written sources simply as elite distortion.[8]

What is historical archaeology?

Despite its undoubted qualities, American historical archaeology fails as an exemplar of how we might best approach the historical past. It does so primarily because of its failure to consider the role of the written word in the construction of power and identity in the past. In this sense, it does not go far enough. On the other hand, in the claim that it is *uniquely* placed to articulate the histories of the forgotten, it goes too far. However, it really goes beyond the pale, and verges on being an exemplar of the 'imperialist' processes it claims to study, when its most vociferous exponents propose that

> historical archaeologists should not be interested in all literate cultures, but only those that inhabited a time I broadly term 'modern times'. ... *This time period began sometime around 1492* (Orser 1996: 27, emphasis added).

This assertion ultimately stems from the second of Deetz's definitions with which I opened this chapter. While this has been accepted by many (for example, Deagan 1988: 8; Leone 1995: 251; Little 1994), most, like Deetz, recognise that their speciality is but one element in the wider field of historical archaeology. Where Charles Orser is (apparently) unique is in his claim that *only* the 'archaeology of the modern world' can be considered historical archaeology. The bases for this rather astonishing assertion are a little difficult to uncover, but appear ultimately to rest on the belief that the modern world is so different from all that preceded it that it merits an 'inherently different', globally focussed, mutualistic, multiscalar and reflexive archaeology (Orser 1996: 15, 192; 1999a: 280).

However, we can argue that *all* archaeology should be 'mutualistic' in the sense that we should seek to understand the network of connections which people created and maintained; *all* archaeology should be multiscalar in recognition of the 'simultaneous relationship of dependency between large scale systems and individual agency' (Hall 2000: 47); *all* archaeology should contain elements of reflexivity, acknowledging that 'archaeology can provide powerful knowledge for living men and

women' (Orser 1999a: 281). Where a 'modern-world archaeology' may appear to be different is in the truly *global* nature of
the processes it seeks to trace. However, while 'globalism' does
find it most extreme form in the modern world, we also have to
accept that the objects and ideas which framed social practice
in the Bronze Age or in the Roman empire must also be situated
within the context of 'world systems' (Sherratt 1993; Woolf, G.
1990). Orser's defining characteristics are not unique to historical archaeology (or 'modern-world archaeology', as he also calls
it (1999a: 280-2)); they should constitute *any* modern archaeological endeavour (see, for example, Hodder 1999).

Orser has a tendency to divide the past into 'prehistoric' and
'historic' monoliths (1996: 15; and below, p. 110), separated by
the overwhelming influence in 'modern times' of colonialism,
Eurocentrism, capitalism and modernity. It is the study of the
ramifications of these 'haunts' which, for Orser, makes historical archaeology distinctive (1996: 22). I have no doubt that these
are very significant forces in the constitution of the modern
world, but again we must question the extent to which their
study distinguishes 'historical archaeology' from archaeology
and history more generally. For decades now, historians, an-
thropologists and sociologists have researched the emergence
and impact of these forces. While it is true that such studies
would benefit from an archaeological perspective, the existence
of hundreds of monographs on the subject surely mutes Orser's
claims to distinctiveness in this field.

Just as significantly, however, one could argue that some of
Orser's forces 'haunted' other corners of the past. They are in
many ways simply the most oppressive and wide-ranging in-
stances of forces which have contributed to the impoverishment
of humanity from prehistory to the present. Colonialism and
Eurocentrism are not unique to 'modern times'. Where capitalism differs is in the truly global scale of its reach and (in this
context, more importantly) in its ability to penetrate thoroughly

to the core of, and thus destroy, pre-existing social systems. I would argue that it owed this ability, in large measure, to the potentialities of the written word. The ability to record, preserve, and disseminate information about the peoples and lands it conquered not only fixed the 'natives' in a new world order, it also facilitated the extraction of their surplus and ultimately contributed to their impoverishment, slavery and death.[9] The paradox of this understanding lies in the fact that Orser proposes to investigate early modern capitalism without bringing into play a factor which was both significant in the reproduction of that system and which contributes to the definition of his own 'discipline'.

In fact, Orser deliberately minimises the role of the written word in both respects. While he does accept that literacy had a part to play in the creation of the modern world, he denies it a 'primary role' apparently because

> many of the individual Europeans who went into the non-Western world were illiterate. The actions of these people and the ideals of the nation that drove them forward were more important than whether they could read and write (Orser and Fagan 1995: 19).

Here he betrays a complete misunderstanding of the importance of writing in the past. Like many historical archaeologists (see above, pp. 26, 102), he seems to see the written word only as another source of evidence – one which is at times valorised and at others dismissed. Thus he tells us that our understanding of prehistory will always be flawed because 'no one really knows what happened' (1996: 4). The difference in historic periods is (of course!) that the *texts* tell us what happened. Similarly, the presence of these texts allows 'historical archaeologists to interpret the artifacts they find in the ground' (1996: 109; also 1999b: 662). Again, the written accounts exist as a *given* through which the, largely mute, objects are made to speak. On the other hand, the voices of the subaltern are deemed absent from the texts and their value for writing 'democratic' history is accordingly diminished.

In this context, the most important point about the Europeans who entered the non-Western world is not that they were illiterate (although this was significant in how they were categorised and defined) but that, like the villagers of Karanis (above, pp. 90-1) they were entangled in the webs of literacy. 1500 years separated the illiterate Egyptian peasant from the illiterate European migrant, and one of the most significant differences was that the spread of print capitalism and improvements in other forms of communications had contributed to the weaving of ever denser webs, binding, defining and disciplining individuals and communities ever more carefully (see Anderson 1991: 37-46).

As I have already noted, the failure to conceive of writing as a technology of oppression (and, occasionally, liberation) is common in historical archaeologies (see above and Chapter 4). Where Orser differs, however, is that this failure is *necessary* for his understanding of what historical archaeology is. In minimising the significance of writing *in the past*, he strategically excludes from his definition all other societies in the past in which writing was practised, and permits himself to blithely assert that Mayanists (for example) are not historical archaeologists (1996: 194; for contrary arguments see Marcus 1992). In effect it allows him to create another 'text-free zone' in which archaeologists can play without fear of contradiction from history (above, pp. 21, 94-5). The problem, however, is that while we can create such 'text-free' zones *in the present*, they will never allow archaeology to really contribute to the understanding of *historical pasts* in which texts were, *by definition*, present and powerful.

Finally, we should note the supreme paradox that someone

who is so interested in recovering the voices of the subaltern and in the promoting greater understanding on issues such as race and ethnicity (Orser 1999b) effectively denies History to the vast majority of people in the past. This is not just because he ignores the role of texts in the social practices through which people defined themselves and others, but because of his propensity to see the past as composed of a monolithic 'prehistory' and 'history'. Historical archaeologists, he asserts, study 'the *post-prehistoric* past' (Orser and Fagan 1995: 14, emphasis added); this 'stands in sharp contrast to *prehistoric*, and is meant to suggest that the world was a different place after Europeans took Western culture to various parts of the globe' (Orser and Fagan 1995: 19). Prehistory thus ended, and history was born, only with the so-called European 'voyages of discovery'. All the peoples of the pre-sixteenth-century past – including the 'literate' communities of Roman and medieval Europe, central America and the Near East – lived in prehistory.[10] The focus on the early modern disjunction separating 'prehistory' from 'history' reinforces the implication that the former was a rather formless, largely unchanging mass – a place without History (see White 1987: 55-6; also Champion 1990; Hodder 1999: 8). Elsewhere, Orser is much more specific and focuses on the date of 1492 for the 'birth' of history.[11] History was thus born with the discovery of America, and here we see Charles Orser playing John the Baptist to Francis Fukuyama's Christ, announcing the birth of History in a nation whose apotheosis was also to bring it to an end (Fukuyama 1992; Moreland 1998: 106).

American historical archaeology has contributed massively to our appreciation of the role of objects in the (re-)production of power, status and identity in the early modern world. However, it, and especially the version offered by Charles Orser, fails even in its stated objectives of understanding capitalism in the early modern world. It does so because it singularly refuses to think about one of the technologies (writing) though which capitalist social relations penetrated other social forms, through which people were defined, categorised and disciplined, and through which production and exchange were intensified. It cannot be a model for other 'historical archaeologies', especially since Charles Orser, at least, denies that they exist.

Historical archaeology is not confined to the study of the modern world or of capitalism. It is not, *contra* Deetz (1977: 5), the study of 'the cultural remains of literate societies that were capable of recording their own history', since this definition focuses on only one aspect of literate practice. Nor is it the bringing together of archaeological and written sources for particular periods of the past. Rather, historical archaeology is a practice which recognises that artifacts and texts are more than just sources of evidence about the past; that they had efficacy in the past; and which seeks to determine the ways in which they were used in the construction of social relationships and identities in historically specific circumstances. This does not mean, as Charles Orser supposes, that historical archaeology has been around for years (1996: 23). There are, in fact, very few examples of historical archaeology as I conceive it (although see Hall 2000). What it does mean is that Mayan archaeology *can be* historical archaeology as much as 'modern world archaeology' can. All we have to do is to exploit the full potential of both objects and texts in the present for informing us about social practice in the past.

Archaeology as text

One of the most prevalent themes in this book has been the 'presentist' disposition of much archaeological and historical thought – both in the focus on the traces of the past simply as evidence in the present, and in the use of theoretical perspectives which impose the present on the past (also Moreland 1998,

2000). In recent years, however, this presentism has manifested itself in a more virulent, aggressive and acknowledged form – postmodernism. While Matthew Johnson (an archaeologist) has recently suggested that 'the question of postmodernism is in many ways a red herring' (1999: 162), some historians are much more concerned. Lawrence Stone argues that its advent has plunged history into a 'crisis of self confidence' (1991: 217), and Richard Evans concludes that only the 'most obscurantist' can now ignore the debate it has provoked over 'history, truth and objectivity' (1997: 6).

Matthew Johnson does not ignore this debate (1999: 162-75), but his rather unperturbed attitude to what many historians see as a threat to their very existence calls for some brief comment. It may be a product of the rather limited impact of 'hard-line' postmodernism within archaeology (although see below, pp. 115-16). Or it may derive from the fact that the perceived muteness and malleability of the material sources means that few have ever expected definitive statements from them – what passes as a serious threat to the historical establishment is part of 'everyday life' for archaeologists. I would argue, however, that, as in all 'presentist' positions, the threat is to the past itself – to the long dead whom it entombs forever, inarticulate, isolated and inaccessible to the present – not to the treatment of one of its traces.

The linguistic theories of Ferdinand de Saussure and Jacques Derrida provide one point of departure for postmodernist historians (and archaeologists).[12] While Saussure noted that the meaning of words was not determined by what they referred to but by their relation to each other, Derrida went further and argued that the relationship between words changed depending on all the different contexts in which they were used. The infinite options thus opened denied any possibility of tying down and defining meaning. Words had no regular relationship with the world and could not truly describe anything in it. In consequence, therefore, nothing existed outside the text (Evans 1997: 94-5; McCullagh 1998: 37-8). There can be no authoritative readings of past texts, since the meaning changes every time they are read. Historians, it is argued, do not find meaning in the past; instead they each read it (differently) into the past. The result is that 'there is no necessary or consistent relation between the text of history and the texts of historians' (Evans 1997: 95; Patterson 1989: 86; also Ankersmit 1989: 138). In effect the histories we write never intersect with the past (Kansteiner 1993: 272).

Our situation in the present and our separation from the past means that we have no means of deciding between the multiplicity of readings (Patterson 1989: 83).[13] For Frank Ankersmit, this leads to the ultimate 'presentist' proposition that 'we no longer have any texts, any past, ... just interpretations of them' (1989: 137), and he concludes that 'there remains nothing for us but to concentrate on the style embodied in every historical view ... *Style, not content, is at issue* is such debates. Content is a derivative of style' (1989: 144, emphasis added). Our engagement with the past, as a search for truth and understanding (both of the past and of ourselves), is thus reduced to a stylistic debate in the present. History becomes the study, not of the past, but of itself (Samuel 1991: 93; Evans 1997: 98). Trivialising the historical project still further, and locating its rationale more firmly in the present, Ankersmit demands that 'we must not shape ourselves according to or in conformity with the past, but learn to play our cultural game with it' (1989: 151; see also Evans 1997: 97).

The axes, saws and hammers of Reformation iconoclasts, and the theologians' rejection of the concept of Purgatory, consigned the Catholic past and its dead to oblivion (Moreland 1999b; above, Chapter 3). With their words, postmodernists consign the whole of the human past to the same fate, remove from us a vital part of what makes us human, and reinforce the 'depthlessness and superficiality' of twenty-first-century Western culture (Zagorin 1990: 266). Strangely for a movement which stems from the political Left, postmodernism rejects concern with the *reality* of oppression, torture, and slavery in the past in favour of *playing games* with their memory (see Carr 1993; Evans 1997: 184-5). As Terry Eagleton argues, 'the political illiteracy and historical oblivion fostered by much postmodernism ... must surely be cause for rejoicing in the White House' (1996: 23) – and especially for the ears of the present occupant.

The assertion that we are in no position to assess the 'truth claims' of different historical accounts means that fascists, racists and Nazis can peddle their obscenities while we play games with style. The logical consequence of postmodernist historical thought (an interesting oxymoron) is, of course, to deny us weapons with which to fight those who deny the Holocaust. This is, in fact, the ground on which many historians have chosen to fight back. Richard Evans demands that we accept that 'Auschwitz was not a discourse. It trivialises mass murder to see it as a text. The gas chambers were not a piece of rhetoric' (1997: 124; also Norris, 1993: 18).

This necessary assertion of truth in the face of the revisionist lie carries with it the implication that the same must be possible in other contexts. In fact, Hayden White, in an attempt to defend himself from charges that the hyper-relativism of postmodernism could contribute to Holocaust denial, conceded that one could, and should, appeal to the 'facts' of the history of the Third Reich to prevent it being written in certain ways (Kansteiner 1993: 293). This concession is an explicit acknowledgement that 'past reality' does indeed shape the histories we can, and cannot, legitimately write (Evans 1997: 125).

Despite their denial of the historical past, postmodernists themselves make 'objective' claims about it. Although Hayden White writes about nineteenth-century *historians* rather than

114

5. What is historical archaeology?

history, it is clear that he intends 'his own historical judgements concerning ... [them] as objective claims' (Beards 1994: 208). On the other hand, they rarely apply their programmatic to their own practice. Thus if everything is interpretation, so is the claim itself, 'in which case the idea of interpretation would cancel all the way through and leave everything exactly as it was' (Eagleton 1996: 14). Similarly, Richard Evans points out that, despite their denial of authorial 'control' over meaning, when it comes to their own works they wish 'to retain their own identity as authors, and their own control over the interpretations to which their own texts are subject' (Evans 1997: 231-2).

Archaeologists who 'indulge' in postmodernism, rarely, as it were, go the whole way. They generally focus on the issue of multiple readings *of* the past and link it to that of multiple voices *in* the past. For some, this reinforces the claim that archaeologists are in a unique position to restore to life some of the lost voices (above, pp. 19, 103-4). Ian Hodder (1999), for example, uses the (rather spurious) assertion that archaeology lacks a common set of aims and methods in order to create a space for the acceptance of multiple pasts and the contention that there are many ways of approaching them. Noting that across the world 'marginal, subordinate, or disadvantaged groups' are interpreting the past in their own terms (1999: 15), he goes on to suggest that archaeologists should relinquish their dominant role in 'creating' the past and become instead 'mediators' who supply

> information, ideas and images to a diversity of audiences from a diversity of pasts. ... Actively engaged in current issues, the archaeologist contributes to a debate, providing narratives which resonate with contemporary concerns (1999: 64).

Some American historical archaeologists make similar connections between contemporary issues and the restoration of the voices of those 'lost to history'. Here, in many cases, this represents a desire for relevancy in the midst of feelings of inferiority and marginalisation (Orser 1999a: 282; 1999b: 661, 665; also below, p. 126 n. 1). Charles Orser argues that to make ourselves relevant to, and reduce our marginalisation within, early twenty-first-century society, historical archaeologists should address *the concerns of the present* by seeking their roots in the past (for a more nuanced argument on similar lines, see Leone 1995).

Here both Orser and Hodder are adopting unashamedly 'presentist' positions. They play to the demands of the multiple audiences of the present, and provide their concerns with an historical ancestry. In some ways there is nothing wrong with this. Archaeologists should take a political stance against oppression and exploitation in the present. Our grasp of long-term history provides us with an awareness of both the ubiquity of oppression and of the specific forms it takes. We can, and should, bring this understanding to bear on current issues (see Leone 1995: 253). However, this is not what is proposed by Hodder and Orser. The issues which concern us today may or may not have been central to life in eighteenth-century America or neolithic Çatalhöyük; the configurations between (say) race, gender and status may (or may not) have been similar. But we cannot *assume* that they were. In beginning with contemporary issues, and not with historically specific circumstances, we run the very serious risk of *overwriting the past* with the present, of substituting our concerns for theirs, thereby denying ourselves not only the possibility of understanding the reality of *their* oppression but also of using that understanding to counter injustice today. As in all presentist arguments, we silence their voice more effectively than did their oppressors.

It is, of course, true that the incompleteness of the record, our 'situatedness' in the present, and our 'methodological naivety' prevent us from producing a single reading of the past. But this does not mean that *any* reading of the past is as good as any other. While we cannot necessarily rely on the restraining effects of the judgement of our peers (Evans 1997: 115-16), our accumulated knowledge of the past and the evidence from the past provide networks of resistance to distortions of 'reality' (Johnson 1999: 175; Moreland 1998: 114-15). As we have seen, even Hayden White accepted that past reality could undermine the revisionist lie, and Paul Ricoeur has urged us not to forget 'the kind of constraint that the past exerted on historical discourse' (1984: 34). As archaeologists and historians, we begin with pre-established frameworks of understanding and, through our engagement with the texts and artifacts, we reproduce and transform that understanding. Through this continuous, collective process we can come to an 'evaluated approximation to understanding', while always appreciating that we can never know the past 'as it really was'.

Another reason why we can never achieve such singular knowledge is because the past itself was multivocal in the sense that the same artifact, building, or event could have been read differently by different people within it (above, pp. 96-7). In the middle ages, Barnard Castle had very different meanings for the lords and peasants of north-eastern England (Austin 1998: 172-206). This does not mean, however, that their experience of the building, and the meanings it held for them, are inherently contradictory and irreconcilable. In fact these different experiences, and the multivocality which flows from them, were linked together in the structures of domination and subordination of which the castle was one manifestation. Here our attentiveness to all these voices, achieved through the kind of close-grained analysis of texts and objects which produces a Geertzian 'thick description', brings us closer to an understanding of how the past might have been for this community (Geertz 1993d: 23).

A postmodernist multivocality is, however, rooted in the present rather than in the past. The collapse of authorial control leaves room for myriad interest groups to assert their exclusive rights to the interpretation of sections of the past, frequently in the cause of reinforcing their identity in the present. It is further asserted that only those who have undergone oppression because of colour, sex, status or religion possess the experience necessary to write the history of blacks, women, the poor etc. The logical consequence of this multitude of histories, based on 'experience' and 'present interest', is that 'no history would be possible, only autobiography' (Evans 1997: 213). More significantly, it would also mean that those 'representing' the oppressed in the present could not, as Richard Evans puts it, write histories of 'white, Anglo-Saxon Protestant males' (1997: 211; also Eagleton 1996: 124). How can we approach the reality of oppression, dehumanisation, and resistance to both, in the past, and bring this to bear on political struggles in the present, if we must speak only of masters *or* slaves, of men *or* women, of Christians *or* Jews?

A postmodernist multivocality fractures the past, and silences its voices, much more emphatically than the division between archaeology and history which is the main theme of this book. It does this by denying that we can ever hear what they have to say, by playing games with their memory, by breaking the complex and variegated patterns of human social practice into isolated pieces, and by desiring only ever to tell (or hear) fragments of the story. The paradox, as I have already noted, is that we lose all this in the quest for a multivocality which is already present in archaeological and historical sources. The walls of the castle speak of both (the need for) domination and (at least the possibility of) resistance; the ridge and furrow field systems of England speak of a daily life of repetition and the exploitation which required it; the texts of Roman Egypt speak of both the demands of the state and the labour of the peasants to meet (and resist) them; the discovery of remnants of the material world of the Catholic faith under the floors of churches speaks of both the resistance which led to its concealment and the oppression which necessitated it.

Mark Leone has lamented the lack of postmodernist influence on American historical archaeology, arguing that it allows us to 'connect material culture with the world of politics' (1995: 252). For the reasons outlined above, however, I would argue that any such influence would be detrimental, not just to American, but to *all* historical archaeologies.

Throughout this book, I have argued that the imposition of the present destroys the distinctiveness of the past. In so doing, we deny ourselves the possibility of understanding the past and of utilising this knowledge to challenge the naturalisms of the present. Historical archaeologies which see objects and texts simply as evidence *about* the past, and which see texts as given, distorted or supplemental, can never produce such knowledge. Only when we recognise that people *in* the past conducted their social practice, and constructed their identities, through the Object, the Voice and the Word in specific historical circumstances will historical archaeology fulfil its real potential both in understanding the past and in contributing to the present.

Notes

1. Fragments of the past

1. As suggested above, and as I will show in later chapters, the dominance of history in the writing of History predates the early nineteenth century.

2. Why these essentially historical questions are more fundamental than (for example) the means by which past populations provided themselves with their daily bread is not at all clear to me.

3. The assumption would seem to be that the deciphered hieroglyphs provided scholars with texts which enabled them to address these superstructural concerns for the first time. However, see Marcus 1992 for a detailed discussion of these 'texts' and the extent to which they constitute 'history'.

4. In 1647, the Leveller John Wildman dismissed the value of chronicles, declaring 'there is no credit to be given to any of them ... because those that were our lords, and made us their vassals, would suffer nothing else to be chronicled' (cited in Thomas 1983: 7).

5. See Cleland 1988: 15 and Paynter and McGuire 1991: 19 for North American examples.

6. This point would appear to have been recognised in the past itself. In 1617, Robert Robinson argued that 'life without letters would be entirely different; princes would rule differently, subjects live differently, and even religion would have a "new course"' (Woolf, D. 1986: 183).

7. Braudel too speaks of the illusory quality of human action, of how the 'delusive smoke [of events] fills the minds of its contemporaries' (1980: 27).

8. On entry into sixteenth-century Europe, they entered into and acquired another world of meaning, one in which they were used as 'fashion items through which elites displayed ... their social status, competing with each other and advertising their colonial possessions' (Saunders 1999: 253).

121

2. Words and objects in the middle ages

1. Although see Andrén 1998: 142; Birkerts 1996; Drucker 1995: 306-8; and Herrenschmidt 2000: 110-11 for apparent threats to that supremacy. Walter Ong provides us with a more realistic approach to computers – the apparent source of this threat. As he points out, 'writing, print and the computer are all ways of technologising the word'; 'writing is a consciousness-raising and humanising technology. So is print, even more, and, in its own way, so is the computer (1986: 28, 48; see also McKenzie 1999: 14).

2. Although I will not deal with this is any detail here, in considering the reasons behind the dominance of history we should bear in mind that many see the use of language as definitive of our humanity (above, pp. 12-13). The survival of 'materialised language' from the past into the present is seen as an expressive link with our ancestors. Clifford Geertz, however, has argued that it is rather Man's capacity for 'thinking as an overt, public act, involving the purposeful manipulation of objective materials' which is 'fundamental to human beings' (1993a: 76). Here, language looses its priority in the definition of our humanity and becomes but one of a series of 'significant symbols' –

> words for the most part but also gestures, drawings, musical sounds, mechanical devices like clocks, or natural objects like jewels – anything in fact that is disengaged from its mere actuality and used to impose meaning upon experience (Geertz 1993b: 45; also below, p. 84).

Similarly, Henri Lefebvre asserts that the

> priority-of-language thesis has certainly not been established. Indeed a good case can be made for according logical and epistemological precedence over highly articulated languages with strict rules to those activities which mark the earth, leaving traces and organising gestures and work performed in common (1991: 16-17).

Such arguments, in conjunction with those that follow, should encourage us to re-evaluate the role of texts and material culture in creating meaning and governing behaviour in the past, and to reassess their value for writing History in the present.

3. I am not disputing the significant impact that the written word had on medieval society. Indeed, one of the aims of this book is to emphasise the power of the Word in past societies (see especially Chapter 4). What I am trying to illustrate here is that people in the past were not as fully enamoured of the Word as modern historians seem to be.

4. Clarisse Herrenschmidt sees this disjunction between reading/writing and understanding as an element in a 'body/mind' dualism introduced by the 'complete alphabet' in ancient Greece. This alphabet, she notes, requires a body – eyes and sound-making organs – and a mind that understands, but does not require them to work together; with the complete alphabet, reading is not identical to understanding (2000: 100-1). For the difficulties in precisely dating this development, see Robinson 1995: 167. See also Hartog 2000: 386.

5. I should make it clear here that we have no definite evidence for the 'demonisation' of Wigber Low. This evidence exists elsewhere and I have introduced it to indicate the transformations in perceptions which can emerge from, and be effected through, the articulation of the oral, written and material worlds.

6. In the following, I will emphasise the positive theological connotations of the Word. However, Biblical authority was also cited against the use of writing. Thus in 2 Corinthians 3,6 it is written that '[God] hath made us able ministers of the new testament; not of the letter, but of the spirit: for the letter killeth, but the spirit giveth life.' Here the 'killing letter' was opposed to the words engraved on the mind and spirit of Man.

7. The belief in the connection between *logos* and Truth was shared with Judaism and Islam (Drucker 1995: 78).

8. For a discussion of the role of inscriptions on objects in the ancient Near East, see Bahrani 1995.

9. We should not underestimate the importance of 'tradition' in allowing the illiterate to read visual narratives. As Marcia Kupfer notes, by the late twelfth century 'recurrent episodes in the lives of confessor saints had ... received more or less standardised iconographies', contributing to the construction of a 'rudimentary visual comprehension' among the *illiterati* (2000: 651; also Chazelle 1990: 148).

10. But as Remensnyder carefully points out, 'inscriptions can be ignored and reinterpreted' (1996: 905, n. 92).

3. The Word and the press

1. Some of the features which contributed to that primacy, including the connection between *logos* and Truth, were already present and appreciated in the middle ages (see Chapter 2).

2. 'Even Bacon, that apostle of experimentation and visual observation, believed that hearing "striketh the spirits more immediately than the other senses", for the ear enjoyed more "present and immediate access to the spirits" than did other organs' (Woolf, D. 1986: 175).

3. For the 'Reformationist' (re-)writing of History, see Jones, E. 1998: 31-54; Woolf, D. 1990: 35-44.

4. 'Logocentric iconophobia' (Collinson 1997: 300).

5. Some contemporaries saw a connection between the process of enclosure and the acceptance of the Word of God as truth. In the middle of the sixteenth century, John Hales argued that people would 'receive, embrace and love God's word' when, through enclosure, they saw that it 'bringeth forth so goodly fruit' (cited in MacCulloch 1999: 50).

6. The urns offered Browne 'physical contact' with the Romans and, as he graphically puts it, 'remembring the earthly civility they brought upon these Countreys, and forgetting long passed mischiefs, we mercifully preserve their bones, and pisse not upon their ashes' (cited in Parry 1995: 251).

7. We should note, however, that this activity was also a consequence of the Renaissance revival of classical antiquity, with its immediate stimulus as 'the restoration of classical Latin and Greek letters through the critical examination of texts' (Levine 1991: 114; Piggott 1989: 9, 18). Equally, we should be aware that countervailing tendencies were also in operation. The iconophobia of the late sixteenth and early seventeenth centuries contributed to a 'more sustained attitude of suspicion toward those who appeared overfond of "relicts" of bygone times' (Woolf, D. 1992: 11; Aston 1984b: 335, n. 95; Llewellyn 1996: 181).

8. It is significant for my argument that the 'ancients' do not seem to have held the written word in such high regard. 'Like Herodotus, Thucydides did not question the presupposition that oral tradition was more important than the written one' (Momigliano 1990: 42; see also Andrén 1998: 120; Gregory 1994: 83). For the middle ages, see van Houts 1999.

9. Levine notes that, in the eighteenth century, 'it was hard to imagine that there might be no written testimony at all, though just when the origin of letters had occurred was then a hotly contested matter' (1991: 72).

10. With Jack Goody and Elizabeth Eisenstein, I am aware that the in-depth investigation of a topic can lead to charges of reductionism and of the use of monocausal explanations (Goody 1986: xv; Eisenstein 1983: xiv; also Ong 1986: 35). I hope that some of the arguments presented here may reduce the numbers making this mistake.

11. It is important to note that the ways in which this written material was consumed differed from that proposed by Protestantism and retained something of the 'medieval' attitude to images. Thus texts were 'sometimes perceived as sources of intrinsic holiness', with the result that the 'printed item ... [became] as much of an icon and object of pious reverence as an alabaster image' (Walsham 2000: 120).

12. In the following, I have supplemented Bradbourne's meagre records with those drawn from elsewhere to construct a 'reality' which, while it might not have been true in all its details for Bradbourne, is a fair reflection of the 'spirit of the age'.

13. I am aware that, in emphasising such contrasts, and indeed in much of the argument in this chapter, I might be seen as 'romanticising' a more wholesome, organic middle ages. I must emphasise that this is not my intention. I am sure that alienation and depersonalisation were aspects of peoples' relationship with the material world throughout most of human history (Moreland 2000). It does, however, seem equally clear to me that such distancing and separation are much more prevalent in the modern and early modern worlds.

14. As Janet Hoskins notes, 'the decline in industrial employment in advanced capitalist countries has meant that an ever-smaller proportion of the population has any direct experience of making things, and there are few elaborate "biographies of objects" ' (1998: 194).

4. Objects and texts in context

1. Interestingly, in Braudellian *Annalisme* even the great and the good are denied real historical efficacy. Statesmen such as Philip II of Spain 'were, despite their illusions, more acted upon than actors' (Braudel 1972: 19).

2. We should also bear in mind my earlier arguments that the growing dominance of the Word and a separation from production have contributed to our illiteracy in reading objects from the past.

3. The theory and its applications are very well known by now, and I will therefore provide only a summary outline of them here. For much of what follows, see Barrett 1988; Moreland 1991a, 1991b, 1997. As Julian Thomas (2000: 2) notes, post-processual archaeology lacks the conformity proposed for New Archaeology by Lewis Binford, and it would be a mistake to see it as a 'school'. Nevertheless, Giddens' structuration theory lies at the heart (or at least at the beginning) of much post-processualist thought.

4. McKenzie notes that the word text derives from 'the Latin *texere*, "to weave", and therefore refers, not to any specific material as such, but to its woven state, the web and texture of the materials' (1999: 13).

5. Human creativity removes the written word from the realm of 'natural' speech and situates it in that of 'artifice' (see above, p. 122 n. 2, and Giddens 1981: 95; Ong 1986: 35).

6. Halverson, and others, argue that many of the cognitive transformations attributed to writing by Goody *et al.* are in fact the product of 'western'-type schools and the use of Aristotelian reasoning (1992: 312; also Briggs 2000: 405).

7. For examples from Mesoamerica and Rome, see Marcus 1992: xvii; Hopkins 1991: 142; Beard 1991: 58.

8. See also Baines 1983: 577; Herrenschmidt 2000: 20, and Harris 1989: 272 for cases from Mesopotamia, Egypt and Rome.

9. 'Written rules surely defined obligations rather more rigidly and fixedly than purely oral agreements' (Hopkins 1991: 155).

10. Writing was not, of course, the only 'technology' used in the production of a coherent world-view. As Mary Beard points out, Livy's narrative history of Rome and the map of empire provided alternative conceptions of the meaning of Rome and Roman history to that constructed by the ritual calendar (1987: 11-12). Here, I would add that the material fabric of the city itself, the actual city within which people lived, provided another such conception (Laurence 2000; Zanker 1988; Moreland 1998: 90-5).

11. This example again shows that writing was not the only discourse used in social practice, and in the definition of elite groups. These written letters were, in fact, accompanied by an oral message and by gifts. The exchange of letters was thus 'a multi-media experience ... [combining] oral, visual and written elements .... Sound, writing and pictures were complementary and essential elements in the process of communication' (Mullett 1990: 185).

12. See Collins 1995: 85; Harris 1989: 215; Hopkins 1991: 145, and Walsham 2000: 102 for other examples of writing as resistance.

13. As Hayden White notes, the ' "history" of "historical" cultures is by its very nature, as a panorama of domination and expansion, at the same time the documentation of the "history" of those supposedly nonhistorical cultures and peoples who are the victims of this process' (1987: 56).

5. What is historical archaeology?

1. This is despite the fact that American historical archaeology has persistently questioned its own theoretical development (for example, Cleland 1988: 13; Deagan 1988: 10, 11; Leone 1995: 252; Leone and Crosby 1987: 397; Orser 1988: 314; 1999a: 274-7).

2. While certainly innovative in its time, more recently details of Leone's argument have come in for criticism. His assumption that the order of the garden would have served to demonstrate his authority within Annapolis fails to adequately consider who would have had access to the garden, who would have been able to 'read' the message (Hall 1992: 383).

3. The focus on gardens and scientific instruments in this discussion is not intended to imply that these were the only means though which the new order was made manifest. Central to the argument of Leone, and other American historical archaeologists, is the contention that 'cups, plates, knives and forks, chamber pots, toothbrushes' and houses were also instrumental in the process (see, amongst many others, Deetz 1977; Glassie 1975; Leone 1995; Little and Shackel 1989; and the papers in section 3 of Leone and Potter (eds) 1988).

4. This is, in itself, a very doubtful assertion since elites certainly used material culture, and the lower orders were certainly used through texts (see Chapter 4).

5. This 'refrain' is also heard outside American historical archaeology; see above, pp. 19, 98.

6. Martin Hall is, of course, writing about South Africa. I include references to some of his work here since it had much in common with the American tradition, although his most recent work (Hall 2000) shows significant moves in the direction I am advocating.

7. Richard Evans' retort to postmodernists' claims that they have been responsible for giving voice to 'history's losers' – 'one wonders what planet … [they] have been living on for the last thirty years' (1997: 213) – applies also to historical archaeologists.

8. Some historical archaeologists do find the voices of the voiceless in written accounts. See Deagan 1991: 100; Hall 2000: 38.

9. Again, I do not see writing as a 'prime mover' in the growth and spread of capitalism; it was significant within, but did not determine, the production and reproduction of capitalist social relations.

10. It is also possible to read this definition in spatial terms; that is as implying that their historical archaeology is essentially non-European. However, this would invalidate its claim to 'think globally' and, in any case, there is nothing particularly historical about it.

11. 'The presence of incipient and eventually full-blown capitalism in the New World after 1492 defines American historical archaeology' (Orser 1999b: 663; also 1996: 27).

12. Here I will focus only on one aspect of postmodern thought. For a simplified introduction, see Johnson 1999: 162-75. For a parody and devastating critique, see Eagleton 1996, and for a detailed analysis of its implications for historians, see Evans 1997.

13. In reality, historians and archaeologists have long appreciated that their 'situatedness' in the present influences their choice of subject, how they write about it, and the claims they can make for its 'objectivity'.

Bibliography

Ackroyd, P. (1998) *The Life of Thomas More* (Chatto and Windus).

Alcock, L. (1983) 'The archaeology of Celtic Britain, fifth to twelfth centuries AD', in D. Hinton (ed.) *Twenty-Five Years of Medieval Archaeology* (University of Sheffield) 48-66.

Alcock, S. (1993) *Graecia Capta: The Landscapes of Roman Greece* (Cambridge University Press).

Anderson, B. (1991) *Imagined Communities: Reflections on the Origins and Spread of Nationalism* (Verso).

Andrén, A. (1998) *Between Artifacts and Texts: Historical Archaeology in Global Perspective* (Plenum Press).

Ankersmit, F. (1989) 'Historiography and postmodernism', *History and Theory* 28: 137-53.

Appleby, J., Hunt, L. and Jacob, M., (1994) *Telling the Truth about History* (Norton).

Arnold, C. (1984) *Roman Britain to Saxon England* (Croom Helm).

Arnold, C. (1986) 'Archaeology and history: the shades of confrontation and cooperation', in J. Bintliff and C. Gaffney (eds) *Archaeology at the Interface: Studies in Archaeology's Relationships with History, Geography, Biology and Physical Science* (British Archaeological Reports, International Series 300) 32-9.

Aston, M. (1984a) 'Lollardy and literacy', in M. Aston *Lollards and Reformers: Images and Literacy in Late Medieval Religion* (Hambledon Press) 193-217.

Aston, M. (1984b) 'English ruins and English history: the dissolution and the sense of the past', in M. Aston *Lollards and Reformers: Images and Literacy in Late Medieval Religion* (Hambledon Press) 313-37.

Aston, M. (1997) 'Iconoclasm in England: official and clandestine', in P. Marshall (ed.) *The Impact of the English Reformation 1500-1640* (Arnold) 167-92.

Austin, D. (1990) 'The "proper study" of medieval archaeology', in D.

Austin and L. Alcock (eds) *From the Baltic to the Black Sea: Studies in Medieval Archaeology* (Unwin Hyman) 9-42.

Austin, D. (1998) 'Private and public: an archaeological consideration of things', in H. Hundsbichler, G. Jaritz and T. Kühtreiber (eds) *Die Vielfalt der Dinge: Neue Wege zur Analyse Mittelalterlicher Sachkultur* (Verlag der Österreichischen Akademie der Wissenschaften) 163-206.

Bahrani, Z. (1995) 'Assault and abduction: the fate of the royal image in the ancient Near East', *Art History* 18: 363-82.

Baines, J. (1983) 'Literacy and ancient Egyptian society', *Man* 18: 572-99.

Barker, G. (1991) 'Introduction: methods and problems', in G. Barker and J. Lloyd (eds) *Roman Landscapes: Archaeological Survey in the Mediterranean Region* (British School at Rome) 1-9.

Barker, G. (1995) *A Mediterranean Valley: Landscape Archaeology and Annales History in the Biferno Valley* (Leicester University Press).

Barnard, L. (1977) 'The theology of images', in A. Bryer and J. Herrin (eds) *Iconoclasm* (University of Birmingham) 7-13.

Barrett, J. (1988) 'Fields of discourse: reconstituting a social archaeology', *Critique of Anthropology* 7: 5-16.

Beard, M. (1987) 'A complex of times: no more sheep on Romulus' birthday', *Proceedings of the Cambridge Philological Society* 213: 1-15.

Beard, M. (1991) 'Writing and religion: *Ancient Literacy* and the function of the written word in Roman religion', in *Literacy in the Roman World* (Journal of Roman Archaeology, Supplementary Series 3) 35-58.

Beards, A. (1994) 'Reversing historical skepticism: Bernard Lonergan on the writing of history', *History and Theory* 33: 198-219.

Belting, H. (1994) *Likeness and Presence: A History of the Image before the Age of Art* (University of Chicago Press).

Binford, L. (1972) *An Archaeological Perspective* (Academic Press).

Binford, L. (1983a) *In Pursuit of the Past* (Thames and Hudson).

Binford, L. (1983b) *Working at Archaeology* (Academic Press).

Binford, L. (1989) *Debating Archaeology* (Academic Press).

Bintliff, J. (ed.) (1991) *The Annales School and Archaeology* (Leicester University Press).

Birkerts, S. (1996) *The Gutenberg Elegies: The Fate of Reading in an Electronic Age* (Faber and Faber).

Birley, R. (1994) *Vindolanda's Roman Records* (Roman Army Museum Publications).

Bloch, M. (1953) *The Historian's Craft* (Vintage Books).

Bottéro, J. (2000) 'Religion and reasoning in Mesopotamia', in J. Bottéro, C. Herrenschmidt and J-P. Vernant, *Ancestor of the West:*

Bibliography

Writing, Reasoning, and Religion in Mesopotamia, Elam and Greece (University of Chicago Press) 3-66.

Bragdon, K. (1988) 'Occupational differences in material culture', in M. Beaudry (ed.) *Documentary Archaeology in the New World* (Cambridge University Press) 83-91.

Braudel, F. (1972) *The Mediterranean and the Mediterranean World in the Age of Philip II*, vol. 1 (Fontana/Collins).

Braudel, F. (1980) *On History* (University of Chicago Press).

Briggs, C. (2000) 'Literacy, reading and writing in the medieval West', *Journal of Medieval History* 26: 397-420.

Buc, P. (1997) 'Conversion of objects: Suger of Saint-Denis and Meinwerk of Paderborn', *Viator* 28: 99-143.

Burke, P. (2000) *A Social History of Knowledge: From Gutenberg to Diderot* (Polity Press).

Camille, M. (1985a) 'Seeing and reading: some visual implications of medieval literacy and illiteracy', *Art History* 8: 26-49.

Camille, M. (1985b) 'The Book of Signs: writing and visual difference in Gothic manuscript illumination', *Word and Image* 1: 133-48.

Camille, M. (1987) 'The language of images in medieval England, 1200-1400', in J. Alexander and P. Binski (eds) *Age of Chivalry: Art in Plantagenet England 1200-1400* (Weidenfeld and Nicolson) 33-40.

Camille, M. (1989a) 'Visual signs of the sacred page: books in the *Bible moralisée*', *Word and Image* 5: 111-30.

Camille, M. (1989b) *The Gothic Idol. Ideology and Image-Making in Medieval Art* (Cambridge University Press).

Camille, M. (1992) *Image on the Edge: The Margins of Medieval Art* (Reaktion).

Carr, D. (1993) 'Review essay', *History and Theory* 32: 179-87.

Carruthers, M. (1990) *The Book of Memory: A Study of Memory in Medieval Culture* (Cambridge University Press).

Champion, T. (1990) 'Medieval archaeology and the tyranny of the historical record', in D. Austin and L. Alcock (eds) *From the Baltic to the Black Sea: Studies in Medieval Archaeology* (Unwin Hyman) 79-95.

Chartier, R. (1989) 'The practical impact of writing', in R. Chartier (ed.) *A History of Private Life III. Passions of the Renaissance* (Belknap) 111-59.

Chazelle, C. (1990) 'Pictures, books and the illiterate: Pope Gregory I's letter to Serenus of Marseilles', *Word and Image* 6: 138-53.

Clanchy, M. (1993) *From Memory to the Written Record: England 1066-1307* (Blackwell, 2nd ed.).

Clarke, D. (1971) 'Archaeology: the loss of innocence', *Antiquity* 47: 6-18.

Bibliography

Clarke, D. (1978) *Analytical Archaeology* (Methuen).

Cleland, C. (1988) 'Questions of substance, questions that count', *Historical Archaeology* 22: 13-17.

Collingwood, R. (1961) *The Idea of History* (Oxford University Press).

Collins, J. (1995) 'Literacy and literacies', *Annual Review of Anthropology* 24: 75-93.

Collinson, P. (1988) *The Birthpangs of Protestant England: Religious and Cultural Changes in the Sixteenth and Seventeenth Centuries* (Macmillan).

Collinson, P. (1997) 'From iconoclasm to iconophobia: the cultural impact of the Second English Reformation', in P. Marshall (ed.) *The Impact of the English Reformation 1500-1640* (Arnold) 278-300.

Collis, J. (1983) *Wigber Low, Derbyshire: A Bronze Age and Anglian Burial Site in the White Peak* (University of Sheffield).

Curtis, J. (1988) 'Perceptions of an artifact: Chinese porcelain in colonial Tidewater Virginia', in M. Beaudry (ed.) *Documentary Archaeology in the New World* (Cambridge University Press) 20-31.

Deagan, K. (1988) 'Neither history nor prehistory: the questions that count in historical archaeology', *Historical Archaeology* 22: 7-12.

Deagan, K. (1991) 'Historical archaeology's contributions to our understanding of early America', in L. Falk (ed.) *Historical Archaeological in Global Perspective* (Smithsonian Institution Press) 97-112.

Deetz, J. (1977) *In Small Things Forgotten* (Anchor Books).

Deetz, J. (1991) 'Introduction: archaeological evidence of sixteenth and seventeenth century colonial encounters', in L. Falk (ed.) *Historical Archaeological in Global Perspective* (Smithsonian Institution Press) 1-9.

Denton, J. (1987) 'Image and history', in J. Alexander and P. Binski (eds) *Age of Chivalry: Art in Plantagenet England 1200-1400* (Weidenfeld and Nicholson) 20-5.

Drucker, J. (1995) *The Alphabetic Labyrinth: The Letters in History and Imagination* (Thames and Hudson).

Duffy, E. (1992) *The Stripping of the Altars: Traditional Religion in England 1400-1580* (Yale University Press).

Duggan, L. (1989) 'Was art really the "book of the illiterate"?', *Word and Image* 5: 227-51.

Eagleton, T. (1996) *The Illusions of Postmodernism* (Blackwell).

Eco, U. (1997) *The Search for the Perfect Language* (Fontana).

Egmond, F. and Mason, P. (1997) *The Mammoth and the Mouse: Microhistory and Morphology* (Johns Hopkins University Press).

Eisenstein, E. (1983) *The Printing Revolution in Early Modern Europe* (Cambridge University Press).

Evans, R. (1997) *In Defence of History* (Granta).

Bibliography

Fehring, G. (1991) *The Archaeology of Medieval Germany* (Routledge).

Finley, M. (1986) *The Use and Abuse of History* (The Hogarth Press).

Flint, V. (1991) *The Rise of Magic in Early Medieval Europe* (Clarendon Press).

Foucault, M. (1979) *Discipline and Punish* (Peregrine).

Francovich, R. (1993) 'Some notes on medieval archaeology in Mediterranean Europe', in H. Andersson and J. Wienberg (eds) *The Study of Medieval Archaeology* (Almqvist and Wiksell International) 49-62.

Frankfurter, D. (1998) *Religion in Roman Egypt: Assimilation and Resistance* (Princeton University Press).

Freedberg, D. (1976) 'The problem of images in northern Europe and its repercussions in the Netherlands', *Hafnia*: 25-45.

Freedberg, D. (1989) *The Power of Images* (University of Chicago Press).

Fukuyama, F. (1992) *The End of History and the Last Man* (Penguin).

Geary, P. (1994a) 'The uses of archaeological sources for religious and cultural history', in P. Geary *Living with the Dead in the Middle Ages* (Cornell University Press) 30-45.

Geary, P. (1994b) 'Germanic tradition and royal ideology in the ninth century: the *Visio Karoli Magni*', in P. Geary *Living with the Dead in the Middle Ages* (Cornell University Press) 49-76.

Geertz, C. (1993a) 'The growth of culture and the evolution of mind', in C. Geertz *The Interpretation of Cultures* (Fontana) 55-83.

Geertz, C. (1993b) 'The impact of the concept of culture on the concept of man' in C. Geertz *The Interpretation of Cultures* (Fontana) 33-54.

Geertz, C. (1993c) 'The cerebral savage: on the work of Claude Lévi-Strauss', in C. Geertz *The Interpretation of Cultures* (Fontana) 345-59.

Geertz, C. (1993d) 'Thick description: towards an interpretative theory of culture', in C. Geertz *The Interpretation of Cultures* (Fontana) 3-30.

Gelling, M. (1978) *Signposts to the Past: Place-names and the History of England* (Phillimore).

Gellrich, J. (1985) *The Idea of the Book in the Middle Ages* (Cornell University Press).

Giddens, A. (1979) *Central Problems in Social Theory* (Macmillan).

Giddens, A. (1981) *A Contemporary Critique of Historical Materialism* (Macmillan).

Ginzburg, C. (1982) *The Cheese and the Worms: The Cosmos of a Sixteenth-Century Miller* (Penguin).

Glassie, H. (1975) *Folk Housing in Middle Virginia* (University of Tennessee Press).

Gojda, M. (1991) *The Ancient Slavs: Settlement and Society* (Edinburgh University Press).

Goody, J. (1968) 'Introduction', in J. Goody (ed.) *Literacy in Traditional Societies* (Cambridge University Press) 1-26.

Goody, J. (1977) *The Domestication of the Savage Mind* (Cambridge University Press).

Goody, J. (1986) *The Logic of Writing and the Organisation of Society* (Cambridge University Press).

Gould, S. (1991) *Wonderful Life: The Burgess Shale and the Nature of History* (Penguin).

Green, D. (1998) *Language and History in the Early Germanic World* (Cambridge University Press).

Greenblatt, S. (1980) *Renaissance Self-Fashioning: From More to Shakespeare* (University of Chicago Press).

Gregory, A. (1994) ' "Powerful images": response to portraits and the political uses of images in Rome', *Journal of Roman Archaeology* 7: 80-99.

Grierson, P. (1959) 'Commerce in the Dark Ages: a critique of the evidence', *Transactions of the Royal Historical Society* 9: 123-40.

Guizot, F. (1997 [1846]) *The History of Civilization in Europe* (Penguin).

Hall, M. (1992) 'Small things and the mobile, conflictual fusion of power, fear, and desire', in A. Yentsch and M. Beaudry (eds) *The Art and Mystery of Historical Archaeology* (CRC Press) 373-99.

Hall, M. (1993) 'The archaeology of colonial settlement in southern Africa', *Annual Review of Anthropology* 22: 177-200.

Hall, M. (2000) *Archaeology and the Modern World: Colonial Transcripts in South Africa and the Chesapeake* (Routledge).

Halstead, P. (1992) 'The Mycenaean palatial economy: making the most of the gaps in the evidence', *Proceedings of the Cambridge Philological Society* 38: 57-86.

Halverson, J. (1992) 'Goody and the implosion of the literacy thesis', *Man* 27: 301-17.

Hamburger, J. (1989) 'The visual and the visionary: the image in late medieval monastic devotions', *Viator* 20: 161-82.

Harris, W. (1989) *Ancient Literacy* (Harvard University Press).

Hartog, F. (2000) 'The invention of history: the pre-history of a concept from Homer to Herodotus', *History and Theory* 39: 384-95.

Hawkes, C. (1954) 'Archaeological theory and method: some suggestions from the Old World', *American Anthropologist* 56: 155-68.

Hen, Y. and Innes, M. (eds) (2000) *The Uses of the Past in the Early Middle Ages* (Cambridge University Press).

Herrenschmidt, C. (2000) 'Writing between visible and invisible worlds in Iran, Israel, and Greece', in J. Bottéro, C. Herrenschmidt and J-P. Vernant, *Ancestor of the West: Writing, Reasoning, and Religion in Mesopotamia, Elam and Greece* (University of Chicago Press) 69-146.

Hill, C. (1993) *The English Bible and the Seventeenth-Century Revolution* (Penguin).

Hobsbawm, E. (1997) *On History* (Weidenfeld and Nicolson).

Hodder, I. (1986) *Reading the Past: Current Approaches to Interpretation in Archaeology* (Cambridge University Press).

Hodder, I. (1999) *The Archaeological Process* (Blackwell).

Hodges, R. (1982) 'Method and theory in medieval archaeology', *Archeologia Medievale* 8: 7-37.

Hodges, R. (1983) 'New approaches to medieval archaeology, part 2', in D. Hinton (ed.) *Twenty-Five Years of Medieval Archaeology* (University of Sheffield) 24-32.

Hodges, R. (1986a) 'Peer polity interaction and socio-political change in Anglo-Saxon England', in C. Renfrew and J. Cherry (eds) *Peer Polity Interaction and Socio-Political Change* (Cambridge University Press) 69-78.

Hodges, R. (1986b) 'Rewriting history: archaeology and the *Annales* paradigm', in H. Kuhnel (ed.) *Alltag und Forschritt im Mittelalter* (Krems Institute for Medieval Studies) 137-49.

Hooke, D. (1998) *The Landscape of Anglo-Saxon England* (Leicester University Press).

Hope-Taylor, B., (1977) *Yeavering. An Anglo-British Centre of Early Northumbria* (H.M.S.O.).

Hopkins, K. (1991) 'Conquest by book', in *Literacy in the Roman World* (Journal of Roman Archaeology, Supplementary Series 3) 133-58.

Hoskins, J. (1998) *Biographical Objects: How Things Tell the Stories of People's Lives* (Routledge).

van Houts, E. (1999) *Memory and Gender in Medieval Europe, 900-1200* (Macmillan).

Hugo, V. (1978) *Notre-Dame of Paris* (Penguin).

Huizinga, J. (1990) *The Waning of the Middle Ages* (Penguin).

Hutton, R. (1996) *The Stations of the Sun: A History of the Ritual Year in Britain* (Oxford University Press).

Innes, M. (1998) 'Memory, orality and literacy in an early medieval society', *Past and Present* 158: 3-36.

Jaeger, M. (1993) '*Custodia Fidelis Memoriae*: Livy's story of M. Manlius Capitolinus', *Latomus* 52: 350-63.

Jardine, L. (1996) *Worldly Goods: A New History of the Renaissance* (Macmillan).

Johnson, M. (1996) *An Archaeology of Capitalism* (Blackwell).

Johnson, M. (1999) *Archaeological Theory: An Introduction* (Blackwell).

Bibliography

Jones, E. (1998) *The English Nation: The Great Myth* (Sutton).

Jones, S. (1997) *The Archaeology of Ethnicity. Constructing Identities in the Past and Present* (Routledge).

Justice, S. (1994) *Writing and Rebellion: England in 1381* (University of California Press).

Kadare, I. (1996) *The Pyramid* (Harvill Press).

Kansteiner, W. (1993) 'Hayden White's critique of the writing of history', *History and Theory* 32: 273-95.

Kerry, C. (1897) 'Ashover. Memoranda by Titus Wheatcroft, A.D. 1722; with a few notes by the editor', *Journal of the Derbyshire Archaeological and Natural History Society* 19: 24-52.

Knapp, B. (ed.) (1992) *Archaeology, Annales and Ethnohistory* (Cambridge University Press).

Kupfer, M. (2000) 'Symbolic cartography in a medieval parish: from spatialised body to painted church at Saint-Aignan-sur-Cher', *Speculum* 75: 615-67.

Laurence, R. (2000) 'Metaphors, monuments and texts: the life course in Roman culture', *World Archaeology* 31: 442-55.

Leach, E. (1983) 'The gatekeepers of heaven: anthropological aspects of grandiose architecture', *Journal of Anthropological Research* 39: 243-63.

Lefebvre, H. (1991) *The Production of Space* (Blackwell).

Le Goff, J. (1992) *History and Memory* (Columbia University Press).

Leone, M. (1984) 'Interpreting ideology in historical archaeology: using the rules of perspective in the William Paca garden in Annapolis, Maryland', in D. Miller and C. Tilley (eds) *Ideology, Power and Prehistory* (Cambridge University Press).

Leone, M. (1988a) 'The Georgian order as the order of merchant capitalism in Annapolis, Maryland', in M. Leone and P. Potter (eds) *The Recovery of Meaning: Historical Archaeology in the Eastern United States* (Smithsonian Institution Press) 235-61.

Leone, M. (1988b) 'The relationship between archaeological data and the documentary record: 18th century gardens in Annapolis, Maryland', *Historical Archaeology* 22: 29-35.

Leone, M. (1995) 'A historical archaeology of capitalism', *American Anthropologist* 97: 252-68.

Leone, M. and Crosby, C. (1987) 'Middle range theory in historical archaeology', in S. Spencer-Wood (ed.) *Consumer Choice in Historical Archaeology* (Plenum Press) 397-410.

Leone, M. and Potter, P. (eds) (1988) *The Recovery of Meaning: Historical Archaeology in the Eastern United States* (Smithsonian Institution Press).

Levine, J. (1991) *Dr. Woodward's Shield. History, Science and Satire in Augustan England* (Cornell University Press).

Bibliography

Levine, J. (1999) *The Autonomy of History. Truth and Method from Erasmus to Gibbon* (University of Chicago Press).

Lévi-Strauss, C. (1989 [1955]) *Tristes Tropiques* (Picador).

Little, B. (1994) 'People with history: an update on historical archaeology in the United States', *Journal of Archaeological Method and Theory* 1: 5-40.

Little, B., and Shackel, P. (1989) 'Scales of historical anthropology: an archaeology of colonial Anglo-America', *Antiquity* 63: 495-509.

Llewellyn, N. (1996) 'Honour in life, death and in the memory: funerary monuments in early modern England', *Transactions of the Royal Historical Society* 6: 179-200.

Lloyd, J. (1986) 'Why should historians take archaeology seriously?', in J. Bintliff and C. Gaffney (eds) *Archaeology at the Interface: Studies in Archaeology's Relationships with History, Geography, Biology and Physical Science* (British Archaeological Reports, International Series 300) 40-51.

MacCulloch, D. (1991) 'The myth of the English Reformation', *Journal of British Studies* 30: 1-19.

MacCulloch, D. (1996) *Thomas Cranmer. A Life* (Yale University Press).

MacCulloch, D. (1999) *Tudor Church Militant* (Allen Lane).

McCullagh, C. (1998) *The Truth of History* (Routledge).

McKenzie, D. (1999) *Bibliography and the Sociology of Texts* (Cambridge University Press).

Marcus, J. (1992) *Mesoamerican Writing Systems. Propaganda, Myth and History in Four Ancient Civilisations* (Princeton University Press).

Messick, B. (1993) *The Calligraphic State. Textual Domination and History in a Muslim Society* (University of California Press).

Momigliano, A. (1990) *The Classical Foundations of Modern Historiography* (University of California Press).

Moore, H. (1990) 'Ricoeur: action, meaning and text', in C. Tilley (ed.) *Reading Material Culture: Structuralism, Hermeneutics and Post-Structuralism* (Blackwell) 85-120.

Moreland, J. (1991a) 'Method and theory in medieval archaeology in the 1990s', *Archeologia Medievale* 18: 7-42.

Moreland, J. (1991b) 'Review of Paul Courbin's *What is Archaeology?*', *History and Theory* 30: 246-61.

Moreland, J. (1992) 'Restoring the dialectic: settlement patterns and documents in medieval central Italy', in B. Knapp (ed.) *Archaeology, Annales and Ethnohistory* (Cambridge University Press) 112-29.

Moreland, J. (1997) 'The middle ages, theory and post-modernism', *Acta Archaeologia* 68: 163-82.

Moreland, J. (1998) 'Through the looking glass of possibilities: understanding the middle ages', in H. Hundsbichler, G. Jaritz, and T. Kühtreiber (eds) *Die Vielfalt der Dinge: Neue Wege zur Analyse Mittelalterlicher Sachkultur* (Verlag der Österreichischen Akademie der Wissenschaften) 85-116.

Moreland, J. (1999a) 'Production and exchange in historical archaeology', in G. Barker (ed.) *Companion Encyclopedia of Archaeology* (Routledge) 637-71.

Moreland, J. (1999b) 'The world(s) of the cross', *World Archaeology* 31: 194-213.

Moreland, J. (2000) 'Concepts of the early medieval economy', in I. Hansen and C. Wickham (eds) *The Long Eighth Century: Production, Distribution and Demand* (Brill) 1-34.

Morrison, B. (2000) *The Justification of Johann Gutenberg* (Chatto and Windus).

Mullett, M. (1990) 'Writing in early medieval Byzantium', in R. McKitterick (ed.) *The Uses of Literacy in Early Medieval Europe* (Cambridge University Press) 156-85.

Niditch, S. (1997) *Oral World and Written Word. Orality and Literacy in Ancient Israel* (S.P.C.K.).

Nissen, H. (1986) 'The archaic texts from Uruk', *World Archaeology* 17: 317-34.

Noble, T. (1990) 'Literacy and the papal government in late antiquity and the early middle ages', in R. McKitterick (ed.) *The Uses of Literacy in Early Medieval Europe* (Cambridge University Press) 82-108.

Norris, C. (1993) *The Truth about Postmodernism* (Blackwell).

Olson, D. (1994) *The World on Paper: The Conceptual and Cognitive Implications of Writing and Reading* (Cambridge University Press).

Ong, W. (1986) 'Writing is a technology that restructures thought', in G. Baumann (ed.) *The Written Word. Literacy in Transition* (Clarendon Press) 23-50.

Orser, C. (1988) 'Towards a theory of power for historical archaeology: plantations of space', in M. Leone and P. Potter (eds) *The Recovery of Meaning: Historical Archaeology in the Eastern United States* (Smithsonian Institution Press) 313-43.

Orser, C. (1996) *A Historical Archaeology of the Modern World* (Plenum Press).

Orser, C. (1999a) 'Negotiating our "familiar" pasts', in S. Tarlow and S. West (eds) *The Familiar Past. Archaeologies of Later Historical Britain* (Routledge) 273-85.

Orser, C. (1999b) 'The challenge of race to American historical archaeology', *American Anthropologist* 100: 661-8.

Orser, C. and Fagan, B. (1995) *Historical Archaeology* (Harper Collins).

Bibliography

Parkinson, R. (1999) *Cracking Codes: The Rosetta Stone and its Decipherment* (British Museum Press).

Parry, G. (1989) *The Seventeenth Century: The Intellectual and Cultural Context of English Literature, 1603-1700* (Longman).

Parry, G. (1995) *The Trophies of Time: English Antiquarians of the Seventeenth Century* (Oxford University Press).

Patterson, T. (1989) 'Post-structuralism, post-modernism: implications for historians', *Social History* 14: 83-8.

Paynter, R. and McGuire, R. (1991) 'The archaeology of inequality: material culture, domination and resistance', in R. McGuire and B. Paynter (eds) *The Archaeology of Inequality* (Blackwell) 1-27.

Peers, C.R. (1927) 'Reculver: its Saxon church and cross', *Archaeologia* 7: 241-56.

Piggott, S. (1989) *Ancient Britons and the Antiquarian Imagination* (Thames and Hudson).

Porter, R. (2000) *Enlightenment: Britain and the Creation of the Modern World* (Allen Lane).

Postgate, J.N. (1990) 'Archaeology and the texts – bridging the gap', *Zeitschrift für Assyriologie* 80: 228-40.

Pyddoke, E. (1953) *What is Archaeology?* (John Baker Publishers).

Rahtz, P. (1983) 'New approaches to medieval archaeology, part 1', in D. Hinton (ed.) *Twenty-Five Years of Medieval Archaeology* (University of Sheffield) 12-23.

Randsborg, K. (2000) 'National history, non-national archaeology: the case of Denmark', *Oxford Journal of Archaeology* 19: 211-22.

Remensnyder, A. (1995) *Remembering Things Past: Monastic Foundation Legends in Southern France* (Cornell University Press).

Remensnyder, A. (1996) 'Legendary treasure at Conques: reliquaries and imaginative memory', *Speculum* 71: 884-906.

Ricoeur, P. (1984) *The Reality of the Historical Past* (Marquette University Press).

Robinson, A. (1995) *The Story of Writing: Alphabets, Hieroglyphs and Pictograms* (Thames and Hudson).

Roymans, N. (1995) 'The cultural biography of urnfields and the long-term history of a mythical landscape', *Archaeological Dialogues* 2: 2-25.

Salzman, M. (1990) *On Roman Time: The Codex-Calendar of 354 and the Rhythms of Urban Life in Late Antiquity* (University of California Press).

Samuel, R. (1991) 'Reading the signs', *History Workshop Journal* 32: 88-109.

Samuel, R. (1992) 'Reading the signs: II. Fact-grubbers and mind-readers', *History Workshop Journal* 33: 220-51.

Bibliography

Saunders, N. (1999) 'Biographies of brilliance: pearls, transformations of matter and being, c. AD 1492', *World Archaeology* 31: 243-57.

Sawyer, P. (1983) 'English archaeology before the Conquest: a historian's view', in D. Hinton (ed.) *25 Years of Medieval Archaeology* (University of Sheffield) 44-7.

Schmidt, P. and Mrozowski, S. (1988) 'Documentary insights into the archaeology of smuggling', in M. Beaudry (ed.) *Documentary Archaeology in the New World* (Cambridge University Press) 32-42.

Schülke, A. (1999) 'On Christianisation and grave-finds', *European Journal of Archaeology* 2: 77-106.

Scully, R. (1995) *The End of Hidden Ireland: Rebellion, Famine and Emigration* (Oxford University Press).

Seip, L. (1999) 'Transformations of meaning: the life history of a Nuxalk mask', *World Archaeology* 31: 272-87.

Semple, S. (1998) 'A fear of the past: the place of the prehistoric burial mound in the ideology of middle and later Anglo-Saxon England', *World Archaeology* 30: 109-26.

Shanks, M. and Tilley, C. (1987) *Social Theory and Archaeology* (Polity).

Shennan, S. (1989) 'Introduction: archaeological approaches to cultural identity' in S. Shennan (ed.) *Archaeological Approaches to Cultural Identity* (Unwin Hyman) 1-32.

Sherratt, A. (1993) 'What would a Bronze-Age world system look like?', *Journal of European Archaeology* 1: 1-57.

Slavin, A. (1982) 'The Tudor Revolution and the Devil's Art: Bishop Bonner's printed forms', in D. Guth and J. McKenna (eds) *Tudor Rule and Revolution* (Cambridge University Press) 3-23.

Snodgrass, A. (1984) 'The ancient Greek world', in J. Bintliff (ed.) *European Social Evolution: Archaeological Perspectives* (University of Bradford) 227-33.

South, S. (1988) 'Whither pattern?', *Historical Archaeology* 22: 25-8.

Spriggs, M. (ed.) (1984) *Marxist Perspectives in Archaeology* (Cambridge University Press).

Stock, B. (1983) *The Implications of Literacy: Written Language and Models of Interpretation in the Eleventh and Twelfth Centuries* (Princeton University Press).

Stock, B. (1986) 'Afterthoughts', *Diacritics* (Fall issue) 74-8.

Stone, L. (1991) 'History and postmodernism', *Past and Present* 131: 217-18.

Styles, J. (2000) 'Product innovation in early modern London', *Past and Present* 168: 124-69.

Tarlow, S. (1999) 'Strangely familiar', in S. Tarlow and S. West (eds) *The Familiar Past: Archaeologies of Later Historical Britain* (Routledge) 263-72.

Bibliography

Thomas, J. (2000) 'Introduction: the polarities of post-processual archaeology', in J. Thomas (ed.) *Interpretive Archaeology. A Reader* (Leicester University Press).

Thomas, K. (1971) *Religion and the Decline of Magic* (Penguin).

Thomas, K. (1983) *The Perception of the Past in Early Modern England* (University of London).

Thomas, K. (1986) 'The meaning of literacy in early modern England', in G. Baumann (ed.) *The Written Word: Literacy in Transition* (Clarendon Press) 97-131.

Thurston, H. (1910) 'The alphabet and the consecration of churches', *The Month* 115: 621-31.

Trigger, B. (1989) *A History of Archaeological Thought* (Cambridge University Press).

te Velde, H. (1985-6) 'Egyptian hieroglyphs as signs, symbols and Gods', *Visible Religion* 4-5: 63-72.

Vermeule, E. (1996) 'Archaeology and philology: the dirt and the word', *Transactions of the American Philological Association* 126: 1-10.

Vernant, J.-P. (2000) 'Writing and civil religion in Greece', in J. Bottéro, C. Herrenschmidt and J-P. Vernant, *Ancestor of the West. Writing, Reasoning, and Religion in Mesopotamia, Elam and Greece* (University of Chicago Press) 149-75.

Wallis, M. (1973) 'Inscriptions in paintings', *Semiotica* 9: 1-28.

Walsham, A. (2000) ' "Domme preachers"? Post-Reformation English Catholicism and the culture of print', *Past and Present* 168: 72-123.

West, S. (1999) 'Introduction', in S. Tarlow and S. West (eds) *The Familiar Past: Archaeologies of Later Historical Britain* (Routledge) 1-15.

White, H. (1987) *The Content of the Form. Narrative Discourse and Historical Representation* (Johns Hopkins University Press).

Williams, H. (1998) 'Monuments and the past in early Anglo-Saxon England', *World Archaeology* 30: 90-108.

Williamson, T. (2000) 'Understanding enclosure', *Landscapes* 1: 56-79.

Woolf, D. (1986) 'Speech, text, and time: the sense of hearing and the sense of the past in Renaissance England', *Albion* 18: 159-93.

Woolf, D. (1988) 'The "common voice": history, folklore and oral tradition in early modern England', *Past and Present* 120: 26-52.

Woolf, D. (1990) *The Idea of History in Early Stuart England* (University of Toronto Press).

Woolf, D. (1991) 'Of Danes and giants: popular beliefs about the past in early modern England', *Dalhousie Review* 71: 166-209.

Woolf, D. (1992) 'The dawn of the artifact: the antiquarian impulse in England, 1500-1730' in L.J. Workman (ed.) *Medievalism in England* (D.S. Brewer) 5-35.

Bibliography

Woolf, G. (1990) 'World systems analysis and the Roman empire', *Journal of Roman Archaeology* 3: 44-58.

Zagorin, P. (1990) 'Historiography and postmodernism: reconsiderations', *History and Theory* 29: 263-74.

Zagorin, P. (1998) *Francis Bacon* (Princeton University Press).

Zanker, P. (1988) *The Power of Images in the Age of Augustus* (University of Michigan Press).

Index

Index

143

Index

Nissen, H. 90
Noble, T. 36
Norris, C. 114

Olson, D. 35, 85
Ong, W. 12, 33, 84-6, 90, 122, 124, 126
oral and written 35-8, 59, 72, 73, 86
Orser, C. 16, 18, 77, 98, 103-11, 116, 126, 127

Parkinson, R. 45
Parry, G. 61, 64, 67, 124
Patterson, T. 113
Paynter, R. 121
Peers, C.R. 48
Piggott, S. 9, 45, 65, 66, 68, 69, 124
Pope Gregory I 47, 52
Porter, R. 69
Postgate, J.N. 11, 12
prehistory 10, 41, 52, 65, 68, 83, 98, 107, 110
presentism 26, 52-3, 78-9, 111-13, 116, 119
printing 57-9, 68, 69, 74, 109
Pyddoke, E. 10

Rahtz, P. 23
Ralegh, W. 68
Randsborg, K. 11, 22
Reformation 54, 57, 59, 61, 62, 73, 74, 113
Remensnyder, A. 38, 43, 44, 46, 48, 49, 81, 123
resistance 30, 31, 39, 87, 89, 93-4, 109, 118-19, 126
Rhode, A. A. 22
Ricoeur, P. 117
Robinson, A. 123
Rogation processions 52, 62
Roymans, N. 43

Salzman, M. 92
Samuel, R. 12, 38, 113
Saunders, N. 28, 121
Saussure, F. 112
Sawyer, P. 11, 34
Schmidt, P. 16
Schülke, A. 18
Scully, R. 62, 104
Seip, L. 28
Semple, S. 41-3
Shackel, P. 127
Shanks, M. 81
Shennan, S. 78
Sherratt, A. 107
Slavin, A. 58

Snodgrass, A. 25
South, S. 78
Speed, J. 63
Spriggs, M. 79
Stock, B. 35, 36, 37
Stone, L. 112
Styles, J. 75, 98, 99

Tarlow, S. 10, 19, 98-9
te Velde, H. 45
theory: 'common sense' 34, 79, 102; contextual archaeology 82-4; culture history 78, 102; Marxism 79; New Archaeology 21-8, 78-9, 102, 125; postmodernism 111-19, 127; post-processual 81-4, 125; structuralism 79
Thomas, J. 125
Thomas, K. 43, 46, 53, 57, 62, 70, 72-4, 89, 121
Thurston, H. 44, 46
Tilley, C. 81
Trigger, B. 24, 78

Vermeule, E. 9, 16, 22
Vernant, J.-P. 13

Wallis, M. 46, 48, 49
Walsham, A. 35, 46, 54, 57-60, 70, 72, 73, 125, 126
West, S. 19, 99
White, H. 31, 110, 114, 117, 126
Wigber Low 40-3, 51, 60, 71, 83, 123
Williams, H. 41, 42, 83
Williamson, T. 60
Woodward, J. 67, 68
Woolf, D. 36, 43, 57, 60, 63, 65, 68, 70-4, 84, 87, 121, 124
Woolf, G. 107
Worm, Ole 11
writing: and Catholicism 56-8, 70; constraining meaning, 48, 48, 82; and the divine 44-8, 50, 56, 59, 84, 89, 91; entangling the illiterate 31, 84, 88, 95, 109; epistemological priority 12, 13, 15, 16, 30, 32, 34, 62, 64, 75, 121; historical specificity 33, 52, 73, 75, 96; preservative power 77, 89-90, 108; socially restricted 14, 19, 20, 22, 30, 88-9; as a technology of oppression 31, 77, 84-5, 88, 91, 104, 109

Zagorin, P. 57, 114
Zanker, P. 126